A Christian Nation?

IVC Publications is the publishing arm of InkandVoice Communication, Columbia, MO.

A Christian Nation?

An objective examination of Christian nation theories and proofs.

David Rosman, MA

InkandVoice Communication

IVC Publishing

Suggested Retail Price: $20.00

This book may not be reproduced, transmitted, or stored in whole or in part by any means, including graphic, electronic, or mechanical without the express written consent of the publisher/author except in the case of brief quotations embodied in critical articles and reviews.

All Rights Reserved
Copyright © 2011 InkandVoice Communication and
David Rosman Columbia, MO

INKANDVOICE COMMUNICATION
104 CLINKSCALES ROAD
COLUMBIA, MO
INKANDVOICE.COM
ACN@InkandVoice.com

Cover design:
 University of Missouri Book Store - Mizzou Media

With special thanks to the late Cantor Felix Burger of the Midway Jewish Center, Hicksville, NY and to Fr. Ed Lasson, SJ of St. Louis University for my religious education. To my mother, Barbara Rosman, who led me into the world of politics and to the Denver Democratic Party to keep me interested in the Reagan years.

There are a number of special friends and people I do not know that without their backing this book would not have made it to print. They all sponsored a small part of this endeavor through www.Kickstarter.com

Ann Edwards	David Wellman
Gini Ingram	Greg Lammers
Gregory Mitchell	Jacqueline Byland
James T. McCollum	Jay Mairley
Justin Lynn	K D Burdick
Matthew Petree	Ted and Rhonda Sturtz

And that you, dear reader, for your purchase.

Thank you all.

Contents

1.	A Christian Nation?	1
2.	Background Stuff	7
3.	Can't Get There From Here	27
4.	The Question	37
5.	In the Beginning	45
6.	The Guys In Wigs	65
7.	Proclamations	95
8.	The Founding Documents	107
9.	God and the Constitution	131
10.	In God We Trust	145
11.	The Court Cases	161
12.	In the End	185
13.	Post Script	193
14.	Referenced Documents	195
15.	Court Cases	221
16.	Notes	223

Chapter 1

A Christian Nation?

ଔଈଊଔ

This book is not meant as an attack on Christianity, though some may believe otherwise. In fact here in the U.S. Christianity is no more under attack than Judaism and much less so than Islam and atheism. So opening comments such as Deborah J. Dewart's in her *Death of a Christian Nation* that "American Christianity is under attack," seem to be more propaganda than truth.[1]

This book is not an attack on any religion. It is an examination of a claim.

The basis of this book is a statement, a thesis, that the United States was not founded as a Christian nation. However, to examine this thesis properly, I must disprove it or at least find the kinks in the argument.

This book is an examination of my own thesis that the United States was neither founded as nor continues to be a Christian nation in terms of our governmental structure or in law. The question that needed to be asked is "am I right?"

To examine this properly, in a comprehensive and meaningful way, this text sought those proofs that would nullify this thesis. The search for objective, quantitative and qualitative proofs that the thesis is wrong; failure to find such justification does not prove the thesis correct. It proves that invalidation could not be found.

To research the statements and positions of those who believe the premise that America was founded as a Christian nation, the original colonization or the writing of the Constitution, or whether the Founders' religious beliefs affected the design of the American experiment, I asked the public for help, specifically for objective proofs from the proponents of the Christian nation positions. I then examined and research each proof to determine validity.

This project began as an idea for two 700-word columns for the *Columbia Missourian*, a daily newspaper I write for in the middle of Middle-America. Once the manuscript reached 10,000 words, the columns were abandoned and the book was started. This started as a personal exercise and ended as an examination of American beliefs, historical myths, and perceived truths.

Yes, the research started with a bit of prejudice. However, that prejudice was discarded every time it popped its head from its hole. A little like "Whack-A-Mole," it was chased back to the depths with threat of a mallet. Throughout the editing, a concerted effort was made to discard preconceptions (as much as possible) and rely on the facts as presented from the proponents and opponents of the Christian nation belief.

The goal is not to convince you that the conclusions drawn here are absolutely right and if you disagree with them you will die. As with the writing by any commentator, this is an attempt to open the conversation to a public forum. It starts with the premise that "This is my opinion and for me it is right. Yours is your opinion and for you it is right. We may not agree, but I will honor your position if you honor mine."

I maintain a deep pleasure in having a reasonable, intelligent and open conversation under these ground rules. You will not find allegations or name calling. I am not attempting any hostility.

My opinions are based on fact, on research, and on curiosity, not on supposition and unsupported claims, not on myths or superstitions that require "faith" to accept. There was no reliance on "documentation" presented by a "reliable source" or reference back to biblical proofs. In fact, none of the respondents provided biblical proofs, only the writings of explorers, Founders and court decisions. A lot of critical thinking and examination went into the discovery process.

These are my opinions and I will support my arguments until someone can provide proofs that I am wrong. Just because one book says something is so is not in itself a proof, and it really depends on the creditability of the author and researcher. There must be other supporting evidence.

Proofs must be available for examination and if based on an experiment, must be repeatable and tested for falsies. This is the premise of my research.

As a matter of disclosure, I am an Atheist, a liberal, and a progressive Democrat. I teach communication, including speech and political communication, on a post-secondary level. I have worked for a U.S. Representative and have been a campaign and communication manager/ advisor for three congressional, one gubernatorial, and a number of local candidate and issue campaigns. This may explain any prejudices that may crop up. It is hoped that this writing has gotten beyond that.

The question now becomes, can I be objective? The late Sen. Daniel Patrick Moynihan said that "everyone is entitled to their own opinions, but they are not entitled to their own facts." That certainly applies here. I am certainly not attempting to create my own "facts," but examined the facts provided in terms of existence, accuracy, context and language of the time in which each was written or spoken. Included are some historical truths about religion, our Founders, and founding documents.

This book is not an attempt to discredit those who claim the Christian Testament as the source of American social and structural life, but to answer the questions concerning the reasons for the original colonization of the New World and the Founders' intentions as it concerned Christianity - or any religion for that matter. The goal is to understand the reasoning of both sides of the issue.

This writing will create a stir among those whose beliefs do not agree with the facts provided, something I have termed as the "Christian nation cognitive dissonance syndrome." Stephen Hawking speaks to "model dependent realism," where our personal reality shapes our opinions and questions concerning our world.[2] Though "facts" may be the same, each side of an argument has a different "reality," so our opinions will differ.

In addition, when facts do not agree with belief, belief wins. Why? Because belief is comfortable, something we grew-up with and have been verified by those we hold important, our parents, teachers and ministers/ rabbis/imams, et cetera.

So why spend the months researching and writing this relatively short book? First I needed to prove to myself that I could write it and, with your help, sell it.

Second, though there are over 150 books currently in print since 2000 on this very subject, none seem to be taking this approach; asking proponents of the various Christian nation theories, each is discussed and answered without relying on "faith."

This book may seem short to some, but, it is very focused on specific proofs, not a complete explanation of the eras, individuals or documents. Like my teaching style, this book is direct and to the point.

గ్రంథంలో

Acknowledgements

I want to thank my lovely Kathy for standing behind me during this project, if for nothing more than to remind me that I am loved. My dear friend Tyree Byndom and his wife Jesca, who are award winning gospel rap artists and hosts of a weekly talk show, "Kore Issues," on KOPN 89.5 FM in Columbia. Then there are my cheerleaders at Columbia College, led by Patti Skinner, the Director of the Evening Campus, my boss, mentor and friend. Jake Sherlock, editor of the *Columbia Missourian* and assistant professor at the University of Missouri School of Journalism, who agreed that I could write my weekly rants for the paper since 2006, encouraging me to continue to improve my craft. David Collins, friend, colleague and keeper of the joke-of-the-day. Dave is an historian and helps me keep things in perspective.

I want to take a moment to thank Fr. Ed Lisson, SJ of St. Louis University for opening up the world of religion beyond Judaism to me. I also want to thank the late Dr. Bob Ross of the University of Northern Colorado for introducing me to the speeches and writings of Robert Ingersoll (1833 -1899).

Michael Adelberg is a writer, fellow reviewer for the *New York Journal of Books*, and the contributing editor for this book. His insight and questions left me thinking about the purpose and direction of the project and what I did and did not want to say. As Michael pointed out more than once, there are many more stories involved that I could tell.

However, for me, those stories would wait for another time.

Carla Burris, writer, editor and veterinarian and all-round good egg. She slashed and burned the manuscript to correct what my dyslexic finger destroyed – grammar. Her friendship, laughter and good heart made her corrections a joy.

Most of all I wish to thank my late mother, Barbara Rosman who led me to my liberal politics, while Don Sheiuer, the former Assistant Minister of the First Universalist Church of Denver (and my "foster" father when my dad, Ben, was 1900 miles away) helped lead me to my liberal religious and Humanist beliefs. And my dad who taught me that hard work does pay off and to do those things you enjoy. My father was not much for reading, religion, or politics when I was a kid. He did own one of the largest single-owner bicycle stores the United States, Mineola Bicycle. His rule was simple, if you have nothing to do, get a broom. (Yes, THAT Benny Rosman.) This project is my broom.

Chapter 2

Background Stuff

An emailed received on August 15, 2011:

> *The U.S. is a nation built on Christian principles, by Christians and for Christians. To yank away all of that influence would be to topple the entire footing of the country. Instead you have chipped away at the foundation and replace the broken pieces with Marxist philosophy. With the help of the ACLU, the goal will be achieved in our lifetimes.* (Name withheld at request)

I do not remember the first time I heard someone proclaim that the United States of American was founded and remains a "Christian Nation." the quote above is one of the milder versions of that argument I have run into. However, since moving to Columbia, Missouri in 2003,

I have heard this sentiment on a regular basis and not only from the fringe Christian conservative movements.

Concerning the premise and writing of this book, I do need to note that I am not and was never a Christian. I was brought up as a Jewish kid in the suburbs of New York City. Today, I claim to be a Jew by heritage, an atheist by belief, and a Unitarian by affiliation. Along the way, I graduated from St. Louis University, one of the premier Jesuit post-secondary schools in the United States, witnessed many a religious ceremony, and there was an attempt to baptize me in the Ohio River. It did not take.

Along the way, I thought about studying to be a Cantor, but decided to become an engineer instead. While attending St. Louis University' Parks College of Engineering, one of four Jews in the school, I was required to take religious education courses. The priest who looked over the flock of 650 young engineers was Fr. Ed Lisson, SJ. The rule at the university was simple; if you were not in ROTC you took a few religion courses including Christian Community and Catholic Marriage. I was also introduced to the Pentecostal Church when I was asked to talk to their children as to why I am a Jew and they weren't. I witnessed people talking in tongues and a faith healing. Years later, I would witness more amazing religious "miracles."

But that did not keep me from going to Temple on Saturdays or from being on the Board of Trustees of two small congregations, one in West Virginia and the other in Denver.

It was in Huntington, WV that I became familiar with various subsects of the Christianity, watched a snake handling service and, again, witnessed various "miracles" of healings, speaking in tongues, and prayer. It was in West Virginia where I first heard that the United States was a Christian nation. It was said in passing and did not set a mark as to why someone would say this.

Years later in a graduate class on Rhetorical Criticism I was an introduction to the writings and speeches of Robert Ingersoll (1833 – 1899), the "Great Heretic." I had a second encounter with Ingersoll during a one-man stage production featuring actor Robert Greeley.

Ingersoll was a hero of the Union Army during the Civil War, during which he raised to the rank of Colonel. Though brought up in a religious household, he married an atheist and he himself turned away from his church. Ingersoll served as the Attorney General of Illinois and was a close friend to both Abraham Lincoln and Samuel Clements. Wouldn't you just love being a fly on the wall to listen to those conversations? It was after the war that Ingersoll joined the speaker's circuit.

Ingersoll's speeches were filled with the three things Aristotle said must be in every speech - Ethos, Pathos and Logos; ethics, passion and logic. They were also filled with questions concerning biblical literature, religion and faith over logic.

The Jewish faith does not believe in a personal deity and I had already started to question if the stories in the Torah as absolute truth. Ingersoll's words confirmed that my disbelief was justified. Or at least were shared. It was then I began my quest for my own faith. I began my question my belief in God. Or gods.

It was in the mid-1980s that a new form of the American religiosity began to immerge. Though other historians may disagree with the timing, I believe the change in America's religious direction began with two events.

First was President Ronald Reagan's declaration that 1983 would be the "Year of the Bible," reinforced with his 1984 campaign address to the National Religious Broadcasters Association in Washington D.C.[1] The public had a whiff that the President was an evangelical Christian, but before this speech he rarely spoke of his faith in public, aside from occasional references to God's blessing on this nation. In private, it was different. We will discuss the President's sentiments later in this chapter.

Reagan was also a staunch anti-communist, believing that communists were all atheists and, therefore, godless. If the communists were godless, then they were evil. This was a holdover from the McCarthy years searching out those godless-commies in American life.

The "no morals without God" argument is not new and as we shall see, was an important element in the presidential elections of 1800 between Adams and Jefferson. It was also a mainstay in this new "wakening."

Today's arguments concerning school lead prayer are only slightly modified from Reagan's complaint. Though some Christians deny the possibility, most non-Christians believe that the prayer is to the Christian God and Jesus Christ. This includes Jews, Muslims, those of no religion, and those whose religions have multiple deities.

When reading and listening to the NRBA presentation, it is evident that the President was saying that the United States was not really a pluralistic government, with secular and sectarian factions sitting in equal thrones, but that American must return to its Christian roots, to a time past when life was better. It was after this speech the idea of America as a Christian nation appeared to expand in the halls of churches and government. It is about this same time when books concerning the religiosity of the nation began to flourish, a growth that continues today.

There should be no question in anyone's mind that the Constitution was not something other than what we had been taught and understood; a secular document that permitted (if not encourage) religion be practiced as to the individual's conscience, and that the government could not sanction religion nor require religion belief on any citizen.

I am often asked, "Why do you believe this way? How can you say that the Constitution was not inspired by God?" It took a while before I was able to answer that question. It is a question I believe we all must ask ourselves. We are who we are because we are brave enough to ask questions and seek answers that just may be in different boxes.[2]

It takes a lot of effort to critically examine the information received from family and religious leaders who told you that the great hand of a mystical and supernatural being was needed to light the match of the Big Bang. Or that a mystical and supernatural being pointed his finger as He created the heavens and the earth. Or that hand belonged to a "he" and not a "she" or "it."

From the worlds of marketing and psychology, numbers larger than five are very difficult to understand. When we look at marks on a board, we do not have to count if there are five or less. If the number is six or more, we count. When evolution is spoken in terms of hundreds, thousands, millions and billions of years, it is difficult for the human brain to contemplate that length of time.

The planet was not created in October 3, 4004 BCE at 9:00 a.m.[3] Bishop James Ussher never did indicate which city was being used and I would think that would be important. Then again, time zones were not developed yet. There is compelling evidence that there were civilizations before 4004 BCE, complete with science, mathematics and written languages.

The writings of Joseph Campbell were the first to open the world of religion for me. In 1996, I received a Qur'an from a friend to aid in my search for a direction and I bought my first of now five Christian Bibles, for my library, which now includes The Book of Mormon, the myths of the Norse, and many other religious writings from Eastern and Western non-Abrahamic sects. The strategy was to study dead religions and those that are very much alive today. I picked books on philosophy, from Aristotle to contemporary writers. Many of my friends and professional acquaintances consider me an amateur philosopher in the field of religion and politics. I consider myself curious.

Within each holy book are exceptional stories, some with morals and virtuous meanings, and many without. Each contained too much mysticism for me to accept as "truth." I found that I really do like Odin, Thor and the rest of the characters of the Norse myths. They could be injured and die. They were more human than not. My next home will be named Valhalla. My cockatiel is Loki, after the Norse god of mischief.

It was my personal discovery of Dr. Carl Sagan, astrophysicist, author, philosopher, scientist and host of the highly acclaimed PBS series "Cosmos," that took me to the next level. The book was Sagan's *A Demon Haunted World: Science as a Candle in the Dark*.[4] It was within these pages the art of critical thinking came to life.

There were three other unlikely books along with Sagan's that helped me form my opinions and my new spiritual path. The first was R. Buckminster Fuller's *Operating Manual for Spacecraft Earth*, his bit different vision of the search for understanding.[5]

While living in Colorado, I met Fuller at a client's ranch where he was to speak. I was invited to stay for the lecture and was fascinated with the way Bucky thought – never in a straight line but always knowing where he was going. He talked about imagination, Einstein, and soccer balls.

Three things came to the forefront. First, believe your gut. Your head can justify anything, but your gut will always tell you the truth. Second, never be cynical but be critical, always ask questions. Third was not to think "out-of-the-box" because there is nothing there, but to think in different boxes.

It is unfortunate that Bucky's book has become so difficult to find, but I highly recommend it to students of philosophy, mathematics and engineering, as well as to divinity students.

The second is Douglas Adams' five book trilogy, *The Hitchhikers Guide to the Galaxy*. (Yes, there is an inside joke here, but you would need to have read the entire series to understand it.) You may have seen the movie, but that only represents the first book.

The series is a humorous tale of science fiction with multiple underlying messages, one of which is brought forward in the guise of the great computer, "Deep Thought." As the story goes, Deep Thought was built by an advanced civilization to complete a single function – to answer the question of "Life, the Universe and Everything." Deep Thought took the question and, well, thought.

99 years later, the great computer announces it had the answer to "Life, the Universe and Everything." The ancestors of the original builders waited in anticipation as Deep Thought warned them that will not like the answer. The citizens did not care; they had waited 99 years for this moment, so Deep Thought took a breath and delivers its conclusion; the answer is 42.

The people were appalled. "*42* is not an answer. This was not a math question." Deep Thought stood its ground and reported back that "Life, the Universe and Everything" was not really a question. And there is the lesson. Sometimes you must know the question before you seek an answer. (By the way, according to Douglas, the mice know the answer.)

The third is *The Art of War*, written about 500 BCE by Chinese general Sun Tzu which, in terms of battle and peace, talks about research and understanding.[6] The General said that if one knows the enemy as well as he knows himself, he will never fear one-thousand battles. Knowing the opposition is a key to any persuasive discussion or debate. As I was being told that America is a Christian nation, or was at least founded as a Christian nation, my logical question was and remains, "Why do you believe that way? Tell me your reasoning so I may understand your position."

The lessons I learned from these books and others would later be the basis of my teaching, research and philosophical methodology for the classroom and for this book. The use of critical thinking, knowing what questions to ask, discerning truth from mythology, knowing the arguments from both camps and believing your gut in times of uncertainty are, combined, the essence of this book.

This does not mean any single idea examined here is invariably right and its counterpart is invariably wrong. It means that we are looking at the same things, the same facts, and have differing conclusions of how they came to be. Neither am I saying that somewhere in the middle is the "right" or universal answer. What I am saying is that differing opinions and beliefs are where discussions begin. Anger only closes the communication avenues.

In addition to our parents, the environment and early learning, we are also be who we are because we are brave enough to ask questions and seek answers that just may be in different boxes.

It was not until sometime shortly after September 11, 2001 when the notion that America was a Christian nation seemed to be fully resurrected in the United States and came to the forefront of my political thinking and my religious education. The first patterns of the resurrected belief and philosophy that God was the overseer during the writing of the Constitution came from a friend who tried a new form of "logic" to encourage my conversion to Christianity. It sounded something like "America is a Christian nation. You are a good American. Therefore you need to become a Christian. If you are not a Christian, you cannot be an American and, therefore, you are going to hell."

This pro-Christian nation sentiment left me afraid that minority religions, including Islam as well as atheism, were somehow being called unpatriotic and un-American. Yet, if America was to stay true to her Constitution, all people of all faiths are to be accepted, with no majority faith overseeing the actions of the minority. Something was, and is wrong with Christian nation line of thought and it had nothing to do with a treat of eternal damnation.

Then new questions arose. Which God or gods do I need to accept, if any? How about Americans who are Buddhist, having no "god" as the Christians, Jews and Muslims have come to know? What about the atheists who do not believe in mysticism in any form? How about those who died before Christ's birth? Are Catholics and Mormons "real" Christians? I am sure they are, though some evangelical and fundamental Christians have told me they are not.

It was this last question that caused havoc to Texas governor Rick Perry presidential bid when Rev. Robert Jeffress introduced Perry to the 2011 Valued Voters Conference. Jeffress said that though former Massachusetts governor Mitt Romney was a good man, he was not a born-again Christian because he was a Mormon and Mormonism is a "cult." You understand why that did not endear the Mormon vote to Mr. Perry.

Why didn't God mention or at least allude to the Americas in the Torah, Christian Bible or the Quran? Book of Mormon was given to Joseph Smith in New York. Was Smith another prophet of the God of Abraham when he was allowed to translate the golden tablets?

When settling in Columbia, I was expecting the typical Bible thumping I had experienced before in West Virginia. In many ways, there is no difference between the two cities. It is just the Christian movements have become more, for a lack of a better word, extraverted.

Since moving to the middle of Middle-America, there have been more proclamations that the United States was "founded" and is today a Christian nation. Many justifications are either biblically based or based on the premise of faiths of the Founders, usually ignoring the concepts of affiliation versus practice versus governmental practice.

Many of the "proofs" sounded good, but a "gut check" said something was wrong. Many of those "proofs" were observational in nature, not a bad thing, but without reference to the historical or scientific facts, not significance. Few of the proofs or justifications appeared to be objective or quantifiable in nature. The many were faith and biblically based.

The majority religion in the United States is Christianity in all of its forms. Of the 228 million adult Americans, almost 173 million identified themselves as Christians according to the U.S. Census of 2010.[7] Catholics hold the lead with over 75 percent of this populous; Baptists and Protestants a distant second with just under 25 percent. But this leaves about 75 million non-Christian American adults, which includes about 3.2 million Americans who declared themselves as non-religious.

The primary proofs provided by the Christian nation proponents include God being included in the Pledge of Allegiance, on American currency and other historical documents, thus claiming that America is a Christian nation.

Many opponents of these proofs use a similar argument as used by President Theodore Roosevelt – Isn't putting "In God We Trust" on our money and coins sacrilegious? Or they refer to the Treaty of Tripoli which states that the United States is not a Christian nation.

As we will discuss later, God was most likely inserted on our money and into our Pledge as part of an American propaganda ploy, first during the Civil War, World Wars One and Two, and finally during the

Cold War. There are few who are willing to use their religious beliefs or God as propaganda. Very few.

Input was sought from people of belief, asking for objective evidence and "facts" to prove their theories right, that the United States was founded and is today a Christian nation by more than just our inherited faith from our ancestral immigrants.

The request for proofs went to contacts on Facebook and LinkedIn (a professional social network), as well as persons in various organizations I subscribe to in both sites of the religious line. The inquiry also went to the members of the Universal Life Church, where many of its members are devout Christians.[8] (Yes I am ordained though this "church," so you can call me Rabbi, Brother, Imam, Sage Dave.)

Over 130 proponents of Christian nation theories responded to the requests, each providing "objective proofs" that America was founded or is currently a Christian nation. Yes, this is a small sampling; however the continuity of the responses provided a base for this examination.

For the proponents "founding" is split into the original colonization, more specifically the colonization of the Massachusetts Bay Colony and John Winthrop, and the writing of the Declaration of Independence and Constitution, using their understanding of the religions of our Founders as additional primary proofs.

The opponents to the Christian nation theories pointed to the same Founders, discussing their faith rather than affiliation. They also use the United States Constitution, treaties and court cases as opposition "proofs."

Both sides used some of the same evidence as their own "proof," thus created a true case for the "Same Facts, Different Perception" theory of thinking.

The question of the religiosity of the nation is nothing new and was argued during the call for independence from Great Britain and during the debates concerning the first ten amendments to our Constitution, the Bill of Rights. The fervor was well noted during the presidential election of 1800 between the Unitarian John Adams and the deist Thomas Jefferson, where the religious beliefs of both men were called into question. Men like Patrick Henry and Alexander Hamilton pushed for a national religion, while George Washington, Ben Franklyn, John Madison and others saw such a move as contrary to the premise of the Constitution, that religious freedom was primary, being the very first freedom and protection in the Bill of Rights.

Though a national discussion of the "religion of the nation" continued, it began to flare again at the beginning of the Civil War, when the Confederacy openly sought God's hand in the war effort. Lincoln would not take this measure until well after in 1864 and then only on the coinage.

It was after the war when politicians, preachers, heretics, and snake oil dealers began to speak in what became known as the Chappaqua Circuit (starting in Chappaqua, NY). Tent evangelical preachers began to equate faith with patriotism and "ungodliness" with evil. Heretics, such as Robert Ingersoll, followed, or were followed, refuting the claims vilifying atheists and non-Christians as not patriotic.

In the 1920s with the advent of radio, and expanding in the 1950s with television, the message of the "United States was Christian nation" used the newest communication device to its advantage. Radio and television preachers used the new mediums to expand their reach and the reach of their churches.

One of the most important innovators of the use of the new medium of radio and television, what would become to be known as "televangelism," was New York City's Archbishop, Fulton Sheen.

In 1928, Sheen found the new radio pulpit amazingly effective in attracting both donations and new flocks to the Catholic Church. The "Catholic Hour" proved to be so successful that in 1951, as television was starting to become popular, Sheen made the move and there he stayed on the air until "Life is Worth Living" signed off in 1955. But this did not stop Sheen or his anti-communist position.

His official web site declares that the Archbishop was not political. In fact it is difficult to separate his politics from his religious beliefs, his deep belief in God and his deep dislike of the godless commies.[9]

To Sheen, his followers and supporters, communism was godless and therefore evil. It was this "atheist" state that was "a dire threat to the nation and the world."[10] Sheen and others made the natural leap that if one was an atheist, then one must be a communist, for all Americans were god-fearing.

This was the same time period of the infamous House Un-American Activities Committee (HUAC). Starting in 1938, the HUAC was designated to investigate persons and corporation who might be or have Communist ties.

It took a few years before Wisconsin Senator Joseph Raymond "Joe" McCarthy took control and the 1952-54 Army–McCarthy hearings began.[11] Being a Communist or an atheist was being un-American. Though Sheen never openly endorsed McCarthy on his shows, they were reportedly good friends.

This was also the time, as we will discuss later, when God became part of America's political language by codifying the national motto and changing the words to the National Anthem and Pledge. We will discuss this later in the book.

Sheen returned to television and remained on air with the *The Fulton Sheen Program* until 1968, closely followed by a plethora of other ministers, priests and preachers. All found the anti-communist stance an advantage to their call. The new electronic preachers would later include the reverends Jerry Farwell, Pat Robinson, Billy James Hargis and Carl McIntire, among others. Each took the same hard line on both communism and atheism, claiming both evil and anti-American.

Evangelical Christianity did not stop with televangelists. During his administration, President Ronald Reagan invoked God's blessings while campaigning for re-election.

On March 8, 1983, President Ronald Reagan addressed the 41st annual meeting of the National Association of Evangelicals in Orlando Florida. Reagan told the organization,

> Freedom prospers when religion is vibrant and the rule of law under God is acknowledged. When our Founding Fathers passed the First Amendment, they sought to protect churches from government interference. They never intended to construct a wall of hostility between government and the concept of religious belief itself.[12]

The last sentence is one I question as to accuracy for the First Amendment does two things. It does, as Mr. Reagan suggested, prevent the government (except in some very specific cases as set by various court decisions) from interfering with an individual's religious beliefs. However, the Amendment also states that the government will not establish or support any religion, again with court cases making some notable exceptions to the Amendment.

As we will see later, Mr. Reagan was mistaken concerning this last sentence for the door swings both ways.

In his 1984 speech, Reagan began with a story and quote from singer Pat Boone, who spoke to an anti-communist rally decades earlier.

ଷ୍ଠାର୍ଥ

Boone, a popular, country, and Christian spiritual music singer, was ranked up there with crooners as Elvis Presley, Ricky Nelson, The Rolling Stones and Paul McCartney. [13] He is also a staunched anti-communist and anti-atheist.

To best understand Boone's religious fever and anti-communist zeal, one needs to go back no further than to May 23, 2009.

On that day, Boone penned a column for WorldNetDaily.com, a conservative newsletter/blog site. He opened his diatribe with three powerful paragraphs.

> Almost every day I receive several newsletters from Christian, humanitarian, charitable or conservative political groups protesting the active, aggressive and increasingly unconstitutional opposition tactics – and sometimes outright persecution – by the ironically named "American Civil Liberties Union."
>
> It's become starkly obvious that this elitist, leftist and subversive organization has abandoned any pretense that it is committed to its stated purpose of protecting the civil liberties of Americans. To the contrary, it is openly hell-bent on ERASING those liberties and, if possible, reinterpreting the Bill of Rights so as to squelch the long-cherished freedoms held dear by most Americans – giving dominance to cliques and minority groups favored by the ACLU.
>
> Apparently, an elitist mindset has completely taken over this activist organization, a mindset so far left that even socialism won't satisfy them; they are determined to re-

create America as a totally Godless, hedonistic, amoral, Sodom-and-Gomorrah-like society – in which there are no rules or majority-prescribed laws, EXCEPT THE ONES THEY APPROVE.

☙❦❧

Mr. Reagan opened his own speech with a story concerning his friend, Pat Boone.

> Some years ago when there was a subversive [communist] element that had moved into the motion picture industry and Hollywood, and there were great meetings that were held. There was one that was held in the Los Angeles Sports Arena. 16,000 people were there, and thousands of them up in the balcony were young people.

> And Pat Boone stood up, and in speaking to this crowd he said, talking of communism, that he had daughters -- they were little girls then -- and he said, "I love them more than anything on Earth." "But," he said, "I would rather" -- and I thought, "I know what he's going to say and, oh, you must not say that." And yet I had underestimated him. He said, "I would rather that they die now believing in God than live to grow up under communism and die one day no longer believing in God."

This was as much a political speech as it was a sermon to bring the Christian faith to the center of American life and to rally the support of Christian conservatives.

Reagan continued, "My experience in this office I hold has only deepened a belief I've held for many years: Within the covers of that single Book are all the answers to all the problems that face us today, if we'd only read and believe."

Yet there was something a bit disturbing in this presentation.

Reagan mentioned the Constitution once in this presentation and that was in context that a U.S. Court of Appeals recently stopped school led prayer as it was deemed a violation of the First Amendment to the Constitution, a decision that would later be upheld by the Supreme Court. Reagan found the court's position appalling and said so in unequivocal language.

> "I think Americans are getting angry. I think they have a message, and Congress better listen. We are a government of, by, and for the people. And people want a constitutional amendment making it unequivocally clear our children can hold voluntary prayer in every school across this land. And if we could get God and discipline back in our schools, maybe we could get drugs and violence out."

Today, many do not realize or do not want to believe that the Constitution and the First Amendment allow for the "voluntary prayer in every school." Reagan's tactic, one that had be used before and since, was designed to take the focus off of the real problems of poverty, unemployment and an inevitable change in the American morals to the emotional argument that without God, we have no morals.

The President was also found of quoting Jefferson's, "The God who gave us life, gave us liberty at the same time." This appears to be a possible error on the part of the President. Not in terms of the quote, but on the emphasis on the word "god."

Jefferson rarely capitalized "god," but used the term more in the mindset of the deist he was. The quote, as written in 1774 concerning the rights of British-American subjects, said,

> The god who gave us life, gave us liberty at the same time:

the hand of force may destroy, but cannot disjoin them. This, Sire, is our last, our determined resolution: and that you will be pleased to interpose with that efficacy which your earnest endeavors may insure to procure redress of these our great grievances..."[14] (Underscore added)

Noting the small "g" in the original shows that Jefferson was not referring to the Christian, Jewish or Islamic god, but to a deist deity. If you question if the lower versus upper case really made a difference in 1774, one must simply refer to other documents of the time. Jefferson did not believe in a personal god, an overseer of daily life. He believed in something that is greater than that type of god.

More about Jefferson later.

Again, Reagan's quote seems at best misleading, at worse, disingenuous to one of the Founders and his legacy.

ଔଔଔଔ୫୦୫୦୫୦

As a possible result of the September 11, 2001 terrorists attacks on the United States, the Christian nation theorists began to argue louder and in earnest that the to be a true American one had to be a Christian and not to be a Christian or Jew was, somehow, un-American. The growth of conservative radio and television commentators increased drastically. Many then and now, as political pundits, continue to stress Christ as the only savior of America and Christianity the only religion.

An unfortunate but common thread began to emerge that the terrorists and all associated with them directly or indirectly were evil and associated with the Devil. The terrorists associated with the 9-11 attacks were Muslim. Therefore, all Muslims must be terrorists and therefore evil. Or as George W. Bush was fond of saying, "evil doers." This unfortunately had a great gravitational affect on a portion of the masses that pulled American Muslims in to the fold atheists and other non-deists and gathered into the hands of Satan.[15]

The reasoning used by some proponents of the Christian nation theories was simple with its own form of Ethos, Pathos and Logos.

> The United States is a great and moral country. To be so cannot happen by accident or social evolution; it must be because God favors the United States over all other nations. For God to do so, Americans must believe in Christ, to be a Christian nation. Therefore, America must be a Christian Nation.

We will later see a similar argument made concerning the religiosity of George Washington and how myths concerning the Father of our Country were born.

The relationship of non-Christian faiths and evil is not new either, but has accelerated with the innovations of the "new" media. A quick Internet search of "atheists" and "evil" will bring almost nine million hits, with more than 80 percent dealing with the topic "atheists are evil." Atheists do not believe in God therefore they do not have morals. Both statements are blatantly false. The number of hits rises to 18 million if you substitute "Muslim" for "atheist."

⋐⋐⋐⋑⋑⋑

This book is an attempt to examine the issue of religion and government objectively. The intent is not to prove this point or that, but to seek evidence to the support a specific view or views of American history. I did not start with a statement that I was right or if I was wrong. I asked for and received objective evidence from both sides, examined that evidence and attempt to show where the arguments may be faulty or correct. As the dialogue on every cop show reminds us, the evidence will lead to the truth. My hope was to find evidence to disprove my own thesis, not to support it.

Notes from readers concerning the various draft manuscripts of this book have suggested that I cannot be 100 percent objective in my research because of my own religious and political beliefs. I do not claim to be and you will find some of my prejudices intermingling with facts and explanations. I would hope you call these comments "opinions" and read them as such.

I train my students in the art of critical thinking and listening. I hope that you find in these pages that I practice what I teach. Though opinions are not ignored, opinions must have substance as a base. I rejected comments that that had no basis or support.

Some may believe that my attempt to remain neutral during the research and in drawing my conclusions is a self-gratifying illusion. I can only ask the reader to accept my personal research ethics that require such a neutral stance as neither self-gratifying nor an illusion. It is also near impossible to be completely without prejudice or bias.

This does not mean you should take the topics discussed lightly. Quite the contrary, all opinions should be based on proofs and evidence in support, and the conclusion made must be based on the evidence provided. If my proofs are somehow incorrect, I want to know.

There are a few who may question my statement that opinions always require proofs and evidence. We all develop our opinions on some factual base, though what those facts are not always easy to figure out or verify. That proof may be a document or something someone told you; it may be based on your own research or from a general interest magazine; it may be only of your five senses telling you something is good or bad. Even one's belief in their God or gods can be traced to its original source, from parental training to the various holy books of the thousands of religious sects on the planet.

Chapter 3

Can't Get There From Here

On Saturday, August 28, 2010, in Murfreesboro, Tennessee, at the site of a planned Islamic civic center and prayer hall, someone set fire to and vandalized construction equipment.[1] This is the same Nashville suburb where, about one month earlier on July 14, there were protests against the building of the new mosque and civic center, claiming that America is a Christian nation, therefore could not accept the new facility.

Glenn Beck and Sarah Palin held a rally on the Mall in Washington DC that August same day, drawing from 100,000 to 500,000 participants, depending on whose numbers you want to believe. Beck wanted to bring "God back into American politics," and Palin cast her wide net of tea party activists to support a strong God and Country platform, in that order.

The immediate suspicion by the press and various liberal groups was that these incidents, as well as the ongoing protests concerning the building of an Islamic center and prayer hall two and one-half blocks from Ground Zero in New York City, were done in coordination with the various conservative Christian movements in order to shift the general elections of 2010 rightward and to influence these elections by using religion as a criteria of eligibility for elected office. Though never proven, the accusations continue and are furthering their trail into the 2012 election cycle.

On face value alone, it is hard to deny the sentiment concerning the mosques and Islamic civic centers. New Yorkers are deeply scarred by the attacks of September 11, 2001. Yet New Yorkers knew about the Islamic civic center in December 2009, almost nine-months earlier, with no protesters in the streets. The center in Tennessee had gone through a complicated public planning and approval process prior to ground breaking. Why were they complaining now? Why so loudly?

Those who oppose the building of these two centers and others throughout the country remain numerous. Their arguments seem to have a questionable bias, uniformly believing that America is a Christian country and Islam is not a religion.

This was reinforced when I was invited as a guest on the FoxFireNews-Online radio show on June 25, 2011. The host, George Sinzer, said that he did not believe Islam is a "religion," using the violence as depicted in the Qur'an as proof. My defense of Islam was pointing out the violence in the Torah and Christian Bible, asking if we need to also question Christianity and Judaism's claims of the title "religion."

Such anti-Islamic statements are based on prejudice and lack of knowledge - or lack of want of knowledge. Of course Islam is a religion as much as Judaism, Christianity, and Hinduism.

During the 2008 presidential primaries, and again in the beginning of the 2012 cycle, the religious beliefs of candidates were questioned, whether the individuals were "Christian enough" as a Mormon. In 2011, we heard the same unfounded accusations made against the same candidate.

This type of religious prejudice within the evangelical-Christian community harks back to 1960 and John Kennedy's speech to the Houston Ministerial Association, stating that religion is not qualifier to hold any public office and that JFK's allegiance was to the Constitution and not to the Pope.

Yet, today many political candidates must express their religious beliefs and affiliation to be elected.[2,3] Don't even think about running for a national office and most state offices if you are Freethinker, atheist, a heretic, or religious discontent.

Kennedy was a Catholic and Catholics were not trusted by the political right in 1960. In fact, distrust of Catholics in the United States can be dated back to the original colonization and further to England.

There was the question if Kennedy would be a puppet of the Roman Catholic Church and remain religiously and politically faithful to the Church. On September 12, 1960, Senator Kennedy was forced to address the issue head on during a question and answer session after his speech in which he had to prove his loyalty to the Constitution above the Pope.[4] He said,

> I believe in an America where the separation of church and state is absolute - where no Catholic prelate would tell the President (should he be a Catholic) how to act and no Protestant minister would tell his parishioners for whom to vote - where no church or church school is granted any public funds or political preference - and where no man is denied public office merely because his religion differs from the President who might appoint him or the people who might elect him.

Kennedy was referring to Article VI, clause 3 of the Constitution which states that one's religion cannot be used as a qualifier for public office.

He would continue to tell his audience that he did not believe in block voting based on any criteria, especially a religious criterion, that he was not a Catholic candidate for President, but the Democratic candidate who happens to be Catholic.

Religion and the office of President continued. Moving forward 40-years towards the 2000 presidential election, the question came up if nominated could Senator Joe Lieberman (D-Conn), an orthodox Jew, have been elected as President on his own accord? Or if his selection as then Vice President Al Gore's running mate hindered a possible Gore/Lieberman ticket's outright victory? Some say "yes."

Today religion is becoming deeply incorporated into campaign speeches and advertising. During the 2008 primary campaigns, then-candidates Mike Huckabee and Mitt Romney made dramatic comments concerning Christianity and the Constitution. Romney had to prove that as a Mormon he was a Christian to gain the vote of Christian conservatives, as he does again in the 2012 campaign.

On January 13, 2008 Huckabee told a crowd at a Michigan fundraiser, "What we need to do is to amend the Constitution so it's in God's standards rather than trying to change God's standards so it lines up with some contemporary view of how we treat each other and how we treat the family."[5]

As we entered deeper into the 2012 election season, God is being used as a lever in the campaigns for candidate, for issue campaigns, and into state laws.

Oklahoma passed a state constitutional amendment barring the use of international and Sharia laws for the purpose of court decisions. In

Muneer Awad v. Paul Ziriax, et al. (Nov. 2010), the Federal Western District Court of Oklahoma was asked if the specific exclusion of Sharia law in a state constitutional amendment might conflict with the U.S. Constitution.[6] The court said the new state amendment was in conflict with the nation's Constitution. As of this writing, Oklahoma has taken the case to the U.S. Appeals Court. Speculation is this will eventually be heard by the U.S. Supreme Court. Missouri and other states are considering the same proposed amendments.

Locally, candidates are using their religions as a qualification for office. A recent School Board candidate in my adopted home town of Columbia, Mo. wrote in her campaign material (even after she was advised not to) that she would bring "Christian, conservative values" to the local school district. She did not win. The same tactic is being used in national, regional, state wide and other local campaigns.

Again in Missouri, the 2011 legislative session produced two pro-religion Joint Resolutions. 2011 HJR 2, the "Religious Freedom in Public Places" which sought to, upon approval of the Missouri voters, add an amendment to the State constitution that would reaffirm a citizen's right to free expression of religion, particularly on government property.

Missouri's 2011 HJR 10, the "Educational Freedom" bill, yet another proposed amendment to the state constitution, would remove "the prohibition against state funds being used to support any religion or religious school." Similar resolutions were and are still being introduced in other states.[7]

In June, 2011, Texas governor Rick Perry issued a call for America to fall to its knees in fasting and prayer for a "besieged" nation on Saturday, August 6.[8] He called for all United States governors and Christian leaders to join him in a "solemn day of prayer and fasting on behalf of our troubled nation."[9] While admitting this is a Christian based rally and national prayer day, Perry rejected Americans United for the Separation of Church and State president Rev. Barry W. Lynn's criticism that his actions represent a breakdown and violation of the First Amendment.[10]

By August and September 2011, religion seemed to hold a special place in the Republican presidential debates, with Gov. Perry and Rep. Michelle Bachman (R-Minn) leading the "I am the better Christian" race. Religion was being used as a justification for anti-Gay marriage and pro-life laws. Though there are voices calling for religious neutrality in politics, they are soft and usually lost in the din.

Though the Article VI, clause 3 of the Constitution prohibits the use of religion as a criterion for holding any public office, many in the Christian nation camp, politically conservative Christians, are forcing politicians to declare their belief in God, whether Christian or Jewish, but definitely not Muslim. This included 2010 senatorial candidate from Delaware, Christine O'Donnell.

O'Donnell talked about her dabbling in witchcraft on Bill Maher's now defunct "Politically Incorrect" in 1999.[11] After the segment hit YouTube in 2010, O'Donnell was forced to publically declare that she is not a witch.[12] Telling the voters of Delaware that she is a Christian and "just like you" may have gone too far-- she lost the Pagan vote and the election.

A 2011 poll conducted by InkandVoice Communication asked the question "Could an atheist win a statewide election for office? How about for United States Representative?" Without exception, the resounding answer was "no." There was almost a universal lack of trust of anyone who was not a Christian by the conservative community. The right type of Christian in some cases.

Back to a few personal notes...

Growing up in the "burbs" of New York City, I was isolated from the ravages of deep religious prejudices. In my community of Hicksville, New York (do not make fun of my hometown's name), neighbors were Jewish, Catholic or Methodist. One of the country's largest Catholic K-6 schools sat around the corner from my home and the parochial high school was a few of blocks away from the public high school.

The neighborhood kids did not care which religion their neighbors and friends were. My Catholic friends were invited to my Bar Mitzvah. I celebrated their First Communions and enjoyed the Methodist wedding of my friend's sister. We all belonged to the same Boy Scout troop. My mother managed a campaign for a Catholic running for school board. Somehow, living 30 miles from Manhattan on "The Island" isolated me and I never understood what the problem was with religion.

Since my arrival in Columbia in 2003, I discovered the "quasi-tolerant" college student, a character I had not met in Colorado in over 20 years of teaching. Maybe it is because I am from New York City or had lived in Denver, both highly diverse and tolerant cities. Yet, in the liberal town of Columbia, I was taken by surprise when two students from a highly respected women's college asked me for money advice because I was a Jew; "All of *your* people know about handling money."

Still another student questioned me about the Holocaust and if it really took place. It seems that his family thought the Holocaust was part of a great Jewish conspiracy to take control of the world monetary fund, or his belief that Jews who did not accept Christ were, therefore, evil. But while he lived in Columbia, he had met many Jews, Muslims and atheists and did not believe any of them were "evil."

He had an informational speech due the following week and I assigned him on to conduct his own research about the Holocaust and to present the results to the class; along with strong suggestions that he contact the Holocaust Museum in New York and to read Eli Wiesel's biography. He did and found that the information he was originally provided was not correct.

A few years later, another student came to me after class at a different school. "My minister said that God is mentioned 54 times in the Declaration of Independence and the Constitution. Is that right?" We read both documents and discovered God is not mentioned in either except as proper for the 1780s in the dates of the documents.

A long discussion of the terminology of Jefferson's "Nature's God," "lord," and "creator" followed. The student knew from her Philosophy of Religion class that Jefferson was not talking of the God of the Jewish or Christian faiths. There were certainly no references to a Christian god in the documents.

She then wanted to know why her minister lied to her. Why would her minister declare that God was mentioned in the two sacred American documents when He was not? I could not give her an answer. I did suggest that maybe he was taught that tidbit of information but never verified the information himself. My student learned about critical thinking and the importance of research that day.

The list goes on and was not limited to the college crowd. I have had adults ask me the same questions, never with malice, but to quench a curiosity. They still do.[13]

Today, religion appears to be more deeply ingrained than when Ronald Reagan invoked God, with some believing that he and Mrs. Reagan also worked with other worldly spirits, to guide his presidency. Some have told me that God had a direct hand in the Christian colonization in America, in the writing of the Constitution and in America's war against the Taliban and al-Qaeda.

Sidebar - I find it interesting that during the editing process, I prefer to listen to Bob Dylan, John Lennon, and Gregorian chants. There is something comforting in knowing that I do appreciate both sides of the discussion.

Chapter 4

The Question

❦❧

During the winter holiday season, I reply to "Merry Christmas" with "Happy Chanukah." Sometimes I receive a smile; sometimes a look of question. Sometimes there is anger.

It is not unusual for me to engage in conversation concerning the origins of holidays and religious and myth practices. I try explaining that Christmas means "Christ's Mass," that the tradition of the Christmas tree most likely started with the Pagan Yule tree and Yule log and, for the record, that there is no such thing as a Chanukah bush.

More often than not, my attempt to educate falls on deaf, if not angry, ears and elicits a deep concern that I somehow "defiled" Christmas. These words echo the same that I heard two-decades earlier from an assistance commissioner in the Colorado Department of Regulatory Agencies.[1]

The greeting did change to "Happy Chanukwanichristmica," a happy mixture of Chanukah, Kwanzaa and Christmas, but that only confused people more than the simple Happy Chanukah. I wish people "Mubarak Ramadan" for during the Islamic holy month of Ramadan. If I knew the proper greeting for Buddha's birthday I would include that in my commentary of greetings as well.

It was after one of these fanciful greetings that a friend pulled me aside and told me that the United States is a Christian nation and was founded as a Christian nation. She assured me that the Christmas tree is a secular symbol and that "everybody" celebrated Christmas.

The conflict between religion and politics in the United States is nothing new. The most recent rise of "Judeo-Christian" nationalism can be dated to William F. Buckley's conservative movement of the 1950s and 60s and the neo-conservatives of the 60s with its resurgence in the mid-1980s. In Buckley's case, the religion was orthodox Catholicism, but as trends tend to move, the Protestant, Evangelical and "non-denominational" churches took the forefront in the campaign to unite God and country. This is the movement we know today.

~ ~ ~

Today's Proofs

Other proofs to the connections between the founding(s) and religion usually appear in the form of pamphlets or the preaching of a televangelist and remain quite subjective. Some claim that today's increase of religiosity in America has also increased the claims that the European colonization and Christianity were the origins of our government. This can be somewhat validated with the increase of religious declarations making their way from the religious to the political pulpit.

The idea of Christianity's priority connection with the American experiment has become noticeably stronger in the form of books, articles, Internet sites, and conservative radio talk shows. The Daniel

Boone Regional Library in central Missouri carries a dozen books directly concerning the Christianity of America and over 200 discussing the proposition, mostly from the proponent's point of view, all printed since 2000. A quick Google search found over 47,000 books referring to "America 'Christian Nation' " since the 1600s, most of which, again, appear to support the proponent's position.

A search of Google Labs' "Books Ngram" shows the term "Christian nation" began to show in books for a short period in the 1650s. There was a revival in church/state connection as the United States entered the election of 1800 with its high point coming during the Civil War, after which a very slow decline emerged.[2] That lasted until the advent of Jerry Farwell's Christian based "Moral Majority" movement in the 1980s and has risen steadily since.

When nation is capitalized, "Christian Nation," the evidence of increased usage is most telling. The term is not seen in print until late in George Washington's second term, and then grows until 1900 when there is a steady decline.[3] However, with the advent of the Moral Majority movement, the incidences of "Christian Nation" used as titles or subjects skyrockets to well over 15,000 books. Clearly not all are proponents of the Christian nation proposition, but the trend needs to be noted.

Most of the objective evidence comes from current readings of history, of the founding of the individual colonies and the adoption of the first ten amendments to the Constitution. There are also references to court cases and interpretations of the "Establishment" clause of the First Amendment, that "Congress shall make no law respecting an establishment of religion, or prohibiting the free exercise thereof…"

By establishing two distinct sections of the first sentence, we realize the possible context in which it was written. That all Americans have the right to believe in whatever god they wish, including the belief in no god at all. Second, that all Americans have the right to be free from any religion sponsored by the government. Thusly, incidents where the church maintains an inordinate measure of power, as we will discuss later concerning Patrick Henry's defense of a Baptist society in western Virginia where the Anglican Church levied taxes, would not happen in the new nation. The third is, of course, the freedom of the press and the fourth to right to assemble and to "to petition the Government for a redress of grievances."

Adding a new level to the discussion is the use of the "Establishment" clause of the Amendment bringing to question when does free religion cross to free speech. In March 2011, the Westboro Baptist Church used this very argument, asserting that their religious based hate-speech is free speech and protects them from certain tort actions.[4]

Westboro Baptist Church of Topeka, Kansas is the realm of Rev. Fred Phelps and his family, who have taken it upon themselves to protest military and other high profile funerals with their extreme anti-gay rhetoric. They believe that God is punishing the United States because of our national attitude towards the homosexual community.

One of their actions occurred at the funeral of Marine Lance Corporal Matthew Snyder. His father, Albert Snyder, sued the church for emotional distress and was awarded $5 million. The United States Supreme Court reversed the jury award claiming the church was protected under the First Amendment's Free Speech Clause. Chief Justice John Roberts wrote in the majority opinion, "As a nation we have chosen a different course – to protect even hurtful speech on public issues to ensure that we do not stifle public debate."

Freedom of religion is tied closely with free speech and without the latter, the former could not exist. It is this tight bond that makes the United States unique and a model for other nations.

Initially, other than mostly anecdotal evidence, interpretations of the Bible and selected quotes from John Winthrop, John Adams, and Abraham Lincoln, few objective proofs are provided supporting the Christian nation advocates' position.

Many take the time to point to the U.S. coinage which states, "In God We Trust," God in our national pledge, and God in the Gettysburg Address. For the three instances above, it appears that God was meant as propaganda, not a declaration of a national faith.

Not fully satisfied that the right people were attracted, the question was sent to members of the Universal Life Church Ministries (of which I am a minister – Sage Dave) as well to Christian religious-leaning groups and general populations on LinkedIn, Facebook and Twitter.

At the time of this writing, over 300 responses have been received and reviewed in my search for proofs that the United States was founded and still is a Christian nation, almost evenly split between those that support and those that oppose the position that the original settlers were committed to the idea of a Christian nation, that the Constitution is based on Judeo-Christian biblical interpretation, or that the United States is a Christian nation today. Arguments from both sides remained identical to those found in readings and earlier research. The objective arguments to the premise that the United States was founded as a Christian nation are sometimes few and far between.

Respondents from both sides of the discussion remained partisan in accordance to religious and political beliefs. The responders who knew my political position discussed their evidence more in the objective style requested.

Those who did not tended to be more subjective in their responses. One, who supported the proposition of American is a Christian nation, threatened that I "better find the right answer" or else. Another wrote, "We are a Christian nation. End of discussion." Those were more the exception than the rule and were discarded.

However, there were well defined proofs from the Christian nation theorists that showed cohesiveness and objectivity in nature. They also had a few important differences.

Research identified that the answer to the Christian nation question depends, in part and when objective, on how you define "Christian nation" and "founding."

When subjective, the responses dealt with personal religious beliefs and one's relationship to their God. Here, there seems to be little if any connection between belief and evidence.

This disconnect was the subject of Chris Mooney's "The science of why we don't believe science."[5] In his April 2011 *Mother Jones* story, Mooney said that "we push threatening information away; we pull friendly information close. We apply fight-or-flight reflexes not only to predators, but to data itself." In other words, during cognitive dissonance the emotional, non-rational portion of our thought process takes command regardless of the facts.

His article extended this idea not only to religion and politics, but to science, climate, creationism, and vaccine dangers and links to illness and disease.

There appears to be a split, however, on political affiliation. More proponents of the Christian nation position tend to be conservative in their political bias. Yet even in this group, there appears to be splits in the concept of the Christianity-Constitution relationship. There is also a higher level of emotion-based argument from the conservative proponents than their religious and political counterparts.

In her October 13, 2011 New York Times article, Sheryl Gay Stolberg examined presidential candidate Michelle Bachman's religious growth through her education as an attorney at Oral Roberts University as she created the connection that "God is the source of law; the Constitution is akin to biblical covenant, binding on future generations; the founders did not intend for a strict separation of church and state."[6]

Of course, the non-theistic groups, atheists, agonistics, pagans and others, balance the scale to the opponent's side. Their arguments range from "Our Founders understood the evils of a theocratic government," to "If there is no God, how could the country be Christian?"

There were also responses from Europe, the Middle East, Asia and the Asian sub-continent. Here, there was a general agreement. To them, the United States presents itself as a Christian nation in entertainment, television shows, news reports, and during interactions with Americans visiting their countries. To many, America does not live up to its promise of a pluralistic government. To others, the United States does not live up to its purported "Christian values." In the eyes of many looking in to our fishbowl from outside, the United States has failed our Founder's wishes -- one way or another.

Chapter 5

In the Beginning

ଓଛେ୪ଓଇ

Defining "Christian"

A "Christian" is defined, for the purpose of this book, as a believer in and follower of Jesus Christ, through not necessarily a member of any specific Christian church. The term, as used here, includes all sects and denominations believing that Jesus Christ is their savior, including Catholics, Mormons, Jehovah Witnesses and other Protestant sects. It does not matter how large or small the sect, or whether or not one believes in the Trinity. The federal government recognizes over 200 of these denominations.

Further, I will not, and cannot, attempt to define or defend a particular Christian orthodoxy. Based on this definition alone, many overseas respondents to the inquiry see the United States as a "Christian nation." One American ex-patriot now living in Germany stated, "...we [the U.S.] are a God-fearing nation," in an attempt to include all Abrahamic religions represented in this country and, unwittingly, including include those of the Islamic faiths.

Unfortunately, as seen in incidents concerning the building of Islamic centers in New York and Tennessee, it may not. We will discuss opinions from overseas later.

Defining "Founding"

Many of those who support the "America is a Christian nation" position refer to the settling of the Massachusetts Bay Colony as the "founding" and John Winthrop's Christian Puritanism as the basis of the Christian's connection with the New World. However, if you look as far back as the first foreign settlements on the North American continent, the reason for coming was to increase commerce and to escape persecution from other Christians. This is not to discredit or disregard the value that religion had in many of these settlements. The New World was also a place, to dump criminals and other unwanted bodies clogging up the streets of London, Paris, Madrid, Amsterdam and other European cities.

Very few define the "founding" back to the British Jamestown settlement in 1607. The 104 settlers, most of who were described by Captain John Smith as "gentlemen" (as opposed to farmers), established a branch of the Virginia Company, a trading corporation, and were motivated to find gold, trade tobacco and locate a passage to the Orient. The settlement was purely business.

Jamestown all but failed with about 25 percent of the original settlers surviving in the first two years, but not for the want of trying. For others making the voyage to the New World, the reasoning was usually seeking a new life, escaping from religious and ethnic prejudice, and evading the law or creditors. Some, like Winthrop, saw the new land as a Godsend, a new Eden ripe for settlement, commerce and religious expansion.

Christopher Columbus

The exploration of Christopher Columbus was not for the religious expansion on behalf of the Spanish church but by the command from King Ferdinand and Queen Isabella of Spain to, "Go west, young Columbus. Go west and find a shorter route to India and China so Spain could corner the market on spices and silk." It was not to spread Christianity, even with the Inquisition going full bore in 1492. The great voyage to the unknown was based on economics, to pay for the wars Spain fought against, well, everybody else who were also looking to find a shorter way to India and China for the wealth so they could fight wars against... The story line goes on for about 400 more years.

One of the pre-readers of this book indicated that Columbus had missionaries on his voyages to discover the route to China. My research did not discover such a manifest indicating "missionaries" were on board though most likely there was a priest or two aboard. In fact, the first indication of missionaries in the new world appears to come from the exploration of Francisco Coronado in 1539.[1]

Yes, Christianity would shortly follow Columbus, but conversion of the original Americans was not the primary purpose. These brave explorers came for fortune, fame, commerce, plunder of gold and a massive land grab, not primarily the spread of Christianity.

The one religion that may have followed Columbus to the New World was Islam.

Dr. Youssef Mroueh claims that Muslims may have been in North America and the islands off Florida 500 years before Columbia arrived on the island of Hispaniola. [2, 3] This has not, to my knowledge, been verified.

Dr. Howard Barraclough "Barry" Fell (1917-1994), a Harvard Museum of Comparative Zoology professor and a self-proclaimed epigraphist, a person who studies languages, is considered one of the "greatest linguist in the twentieth century," at least by some. In his book *Saga America*, Fell claims that he found evidence, through language and other linguistic artifacts, that the origins of many words in the Native American languages were Arabic and, therefore, an Arab influence in the New World pre-dating Columbus.[4] However, archeologists, linguists and others who have studied the history of Islam in the New World dispute Fell's and Mroueh's conclusions. [5] Again, collaborating evidence was not found.

There is a real possibility that when Columbus sailed the oceans blue in 1492, Muslims were an important part of the trip's complement of sailors and navigators. We know that Muslim brothers Martin Alonso and Vicente Yáñez Pinzón captained the Pinta and Niña respectively, and a third brother, Francisco Martín Pinzón, was the master of the Pinta.

The claim is that they were from the "Moroccan Marinid dynasty, descendants of Sultan Abu Zayan Muhammad III (r. 1362-1366). Formerly well-to-do ship riggers, these three assisted Columbus in organizing his voyage of exploration, preparing the Santa Maria, the flagship, and covering all its expenses."[6] Whether they were still practicing Muslims or had converted to Christianity by 1492 is not known.

೧೫೦೮೦೦೩

Puritans, Pilgrims, and Massachusetts

There are four terms that need to be defined before a discussion concerning Massachusetts can continue: Pilgrim and pilgrim, Puritan and puritan.[7]

A pilgrim, with a lower case "p," is a person or group of persons who have made a trek to a holy or religiously significant site. The

Pilgrims, with the upper case "P," represents those who traveled to the New World, settling and establishing the colony at Plymouth.

A puritan, again with a lower case "p," is a member of a sect of Christians who wanted to bring their Church back to the "pure" form of Christianity. The settlers at Plymouth were indeed puritans. However, with an upper case "P," the term 'Puritans' indicates members/residents of the settlement established by John Winthrop, Boston.

The confusion concerning who landed and ruled each of these two settlements and when they were founded is not unusual, except possibly to those who live in New England or who claim direct ancestry as Mayflower descendants. However, the settlements at Boston and Plymouth, separated by a decade, produced two important documents.

Reading *A Magnificent Catastrophe: The Tumultuous Election of 1800, America's First Presidential Campaign*, by Edward Larson, one begins to understand that one's beliefs were very much a part of the election process from the beginning. The political dispute concerning religion and government in the New World can be traced back to the Massachusetts Bay Colony, the Puritans, and John Winthrop, the religious and political leader of the new colony. Today, John Winthrop would be called a, orthodox fundamentalist Christian.

When discussing religious freedom today, the Massachusetts Bay Colony and John Winthrop are usually placed as the Christian foundation in the New World. With our knowledge of the colony today, it is difficult at best to accept that the Puritan leader was a champion of religious freedom just because he left European and English persecution to save his faith. That he did. However, the main purpose of the new settlement was for commerce, while invoking God to bless the success of the new settlement.

In 1630, during the voyage from England to the new World,

Winthrop wrote a sermon on his flagship, the Arbella (one of eleven ships making the voyage), "A Modell for Christian Charity." It is this sermon to which many of the Proponents of the Christian nation theories deem as the basis of the United States being a Christian nation, believing that the Puritans landing at what became Boston was the "founding" of the new nation.

Unfortunately, Winthrop created a settlement that was as intolerant, if not more so, of other beliefs (and ethnicities) as Europe had been of theirs. Winthrop's agreement with England was, as described by historian Michael Adelberg, a "quid-pro-quo," allowing the Puritans to resettle and practice their beliefs within their compound without persecution from the Mother Country.

In fact, it was not Winthrop who first to establish a puritan settlement in Massachusetts. Ten years before Winthrop's arrival, William Bradford, did arrive on the original *Mayflower* (A second *Mayflower* was part of Winthrop's fleet.), establishing the Plymouth Colony. The document that was written on the *Mayflower*, "The Compact" allowed the Pilgrims to settle and practice their religion in exchange for commerce. Today most Americans seem to combine the two events; the founding of Plymouth and the founding of the Boston.

Plymouth and Boston were both religiously puritan settlements and both groups believed that the Anglican Church had not gone far enough in its separation from the Catholic Church in 1535. Plymouth was founded first with the arrival of the *Mayflower* in 1620 with William Bradford, calling themselves Pilgrims, a term to denote their search for a new land.

John Winthrop's settlement of Boston began in 1630[*], establishing

---

[*] Explorer John Cabot was the first to known European to sail the Massachusetts coast in 1498, with Bartholomew Gosnold exploring the New England coast line in 1602.

its own enclave with strict biblical rules and laws as understood by this sect of puritans. This new set of "rules" was apparently much stricter than those of the Pilgrims in Plymouth, though not dissimilar.

The puritan biblical laws led to actions against those who believed differently and, as they were defined by Winthrop, were so extremely inflexible that fellow puritan leader Roger Williams was kicked out because he dared suggest that temporal law and biblical law were different, that the confiscation of Native American lands without compensation was immoral, and the punishment of purely religious transgressions by the civil officials was not right.

It was Williams who founded the colony of Rhode Island and Providence Plantations in 1663. It must be noted that Winthrop assisted Williams in acquiring the Rhode Island charter.

Today, Winthrop's *City on a Hill* speech is often cited as proof that the United States was founded as a Christian nation. The fact does remain that the Charter for the Massachusetts Bay Colony was awarded as much for the commerce as it was for England and Europe to be rid of those annoying Puritans. It must also be noted that the charter received by Williams and Winthrop were for the settlements only. Is this not the same Boston that in the 16th and 17th centuries where witches and other heretics were put on trial, burned, drowned, or otherwise disposed?

☙❦❧

Mayflower Compact

This document was written on the *Mayflower* and is considered the model of the government for the new settlement of New Plymouth. Known as the *Mayflower Compact of November 11, 1620*, it was written ten years before John Winthrop landed in the new world aboard the *Arbella*, and was not a sectarian document, though it contained the language of religion as was common in the 1620s.

Governor William Bradford saw that there was no discipline, no "unity and concord" among those on the *Mayflower* and foresaw the colony failing before it began. He knew that there had to be a formal document to gain order and management. Bradford set the rules for the governing of the new settlement, not as a Christian colony but as a colony of temporal governance.

After the formalities of the time, praising the King, God and country, Bradford wrote:

> "...do by these presents solemnly and mutually in the presence of God, and one of another, covenant and combine ourselves together into a *civil body politic*, for our better ordering and preservation and furtherance of the ends aforesaid; and by virtue hereof to enact, constitute, and frame such just and equal laws, ordinances, acts, constitutions, and offices, from time to time, as shall be thought most meet and convenient for the general good of the colony, unto which we promise all due submission and obedience."[8] (Italics added)

All 41 men aboard the *Mayflower* signed the Compact and it became the law of the land.

This is a short document, under 200 words, that attempted but would later fail to complete the allure of an open and free citizenry in the Plymouth settlement.

There is a valid argument that the Compact does talk to "Having undertaken for the Glory of God, and Advancement of the Christian Faith..." As a standalone statement, the argument seems proper, however, there is no clear indication whether this meant that the language was there as 1) traditional and accepted language of the day (most likely), 2) concerning the advancement and growth of an orthodox Christian settlement, or 3) the conversion of the people of the citizens of the Massachusetts Confederacy of Nations, from which the colony was named and included the native American nations of all of modern New England, including the approximately 12,000 Wampanoag people who inhabited most of today's southeast Massachusetts.

The new settlement was to be a "civil body politic," not a theocratic body politic as many Christian nation proponents surmise in their notes and emails. The laws set forth in this document were the laws of man, not those of the Bible; though, as we have seen, this would not last long.

The Compact was initially replaced by the 1621 Peirce Patent, which gave the colonists greater freedoms and control of their own future. It was not until 1629 when Winthrop and the Puritans gained their Charter for a colony did things change.

So important was the Mayflower Compact that in 1802 future president John Quincy Adams, himself a descendent of the ship's passengers, declared the document was the basis of the American Constitution.

CB☙❧CR

A Modell of a Christian Charity or "The City upon a Hill"

John Winthrop, who was labeled a "non-conformist" and a heretic by other Christians in Europe, may not have been the only leader of a New World settlement who proclaimed America to be the "New Eden," but he was the first to dedicate the rule of the colony based on Christian beliefs. Winthrop's "laws" were as intolerant, if not more so, of others' differing interpretations of the Christian Bible as Protestant and Catholic Europe's were of his interpretations.

Many Christian nation proponents cite this as Winthrop's "City Upon a Hill" and as proof positive the founding of the Massachusetts Bay Colony was based on Christianity. However, "City upon a Hill" represents only the last paragraphs of the entire document and does not stand alone. By itself, these paragraphs would indicate that Winthrop's vision was truly a theocratic settlement.

"City upon a Hill" was quoted by Ronald Reagan and Mario Cuomo in their respective 1984 political party convention keynote addresses. This, as we will see later, may be one of the six to ten "happenings" that started the modern version of the Christian nation movement.

The document was Winthrop's vision for the new settlement and is a listing of rules, that some would later call a treatise, on board the Arbella in 1630, was appropriately titled "A Modell of a Christian Charity," and is one of the first times the notion that any territory of the New World would be dedicated to Christianity.[9] It was unfortunate that the puritan denomination had little if any tolerance for dissenters of the faith as prescribed by Winthrop.

Winthrop's document reflected the beliefs of one man and his loyal following. Unlike Bradford's Mayflower Compact, "A Modell" was not signed by settlers onboard the Arbella. However, the settlers did obey their spiritual and exploration leader without question and all were devout and, what I term today, orthodox Christians.

In his sermon, "A Modell for a Christian Charity," Winthrop said,

> There are two rules whereby we are to walk one towards another: Justice and Mercy. These are always distinguished in their act and in their object, yet may they both concur in the same subject in each respect; as sometimes there may be an occasion of showing mercy to a rich man in some sudden danger or distress, and also doing of mere justice to a poor man in regard of some

particular contract, etc.

Winthrop gave three "Reasons" to justify his two rules. The first was to praise God for the bounty of the planet. The second was to ask God for his mercy on the poor, the wicked and to ask that all would strive, "in exercising His graces in them, as in the great ones, their love, mercy, gentleness, temperance etc., and in the poor and inferior sort, their faith, patience, obedience etc." and survive this ordeal.

The third reason, though justified through biblical passages, was more temporal.

> Thirdly, that every man might have need of others and from hence they might be all knit more nearly together in the bonds of brotherly affection. From hence it appears plainly that no man is made more honorable than another or more wealthy etc., out of any particular and singular respect to himself, but for the glory of his Creator and the common good of the creature, man... All men being thus (by divine providence) ranked into two sorts, rich and poor; under the first are comprehended all such as are able to live comfortably by their own means duly improved; and all others are poor according to the former distribution.

Not exactly in accordance of Christian values as we know them today, but this strongly indicates that Winthrop's ideal of a Christian nation was based on laws conceived by and followed by man.

The puritans believed that God sent them to New England to find a settlement espousing "A Modell of Christian Charity." One of the final paragraphs of "A Modell" says,

> Wee shall finde that the God of Israell is among us, when ten of us shall be able to resist a thousand of our

enemies; when hee shall make us a prayse and glory that men shall say of succeeding plantations, "the Lord make it likely that of New England." For wee must consider that wee shall be as a citty upon a hill. The eies of all people are uppon us. Soe that if wee shall deale falsely with our God in this worke wee haue undertaken, and soe cause him to withdrawe his present help from us, wee shall be made a story and a by-word through the world. Wee shall open the mouthes of enemies to speake evill of the wayes of God, and all professors for God's sake. Wee shall shame the faces of many of God's worthy servants, and cause theire prayers to be turned into curses upon us till wee be consumed out of the good land whither wee are a goeing.

History would eventually prove otherwise. Intolerance in the Massachusetts Bay Colony was, and is still, a black mark on New England's history.

It is this selective reading and interpretation of early American history that causes the rift between the promoters of the Christian nation position and many of the opponents.

Winthrop's displeasures, however, came from those who had more liberal translations of scripture and other acts of heresy. There are two noted incidents here. First was the banishing of Roger Williams from the colony and the founding of Rhode Island and Providence Plantation colony, the most religiously tolerant colony of the time. But this was not the first series of attacks based on heresy. The second concerned a third settlement in Massachusetts, Ma-re Mount (pronounced Merry Mount), a Pagan settlement.

Rhode Island and Providence Plantation

Williams' heresy in Plymouth was to proclaim, based on his interpretation of Matthew 22:15 in which Jesus said "Give to Caesar what is Caesar's, and to God what is God's," that the laws of the Church and the laws of man were separate and equal partners.[10] It was in Rhode Island and the Providence Plantation that the New World saw the first permanent Jewish community and synagogue in the American colonies.

The colony of Rhode Island and Providence Plantation was "...a body corporate and politic, in fact and name, by the name of The Governor and Company of the English Colony of Rhode-Island and Providence Plantations, in New-England, in America."[11] There was no requirement to establish a state religion, though Rhode Island, as did all other colonies, eventually would. It appears from the language of the charter that a state sponsored religion may in fact been discouraged.

Rhode Island and Providence Plantation was the New World's first true pluralistic government to be chartered by the British Empire, a tolerant society making a break from Winthrop's puritan ideals of pure Christianity.

The 1633 Charter of Rhode Island and Providence Plantation specifically ordered,

> ...that noe person within the sayd colonye, at any tyme hereafter, shall bee any wise molested, punished, disquieted, or called in question, for any differences in opinione in matters of religion, and doe not actually disturb the civill peace of our sayd colony; but that all and everye person and persons may, from tyme to tyme, and at all tymes hereafter, freelye and fullye have and enjoye his and theire owne judgments and consciences, in matters of religious concernments...[12]

Tolerance was so important to the new colony that Touro Synagogue was permitted to be establish in Newport, Rhode Island in 1658. The ground breaking for the formal house of worship, the synagogue, began in 1758 with the synagogue dedication in 1763. Touro Synagogue still hosts an active and vibrant congregation over 350 years later.[13]

This is the same synagogue that wrote to George Washington to expressing their gratitude in the freedom of religious sanctity for all beliefs, and to thank Washington for his support of the First Amendment to the Constitution.

In 1790, Moses Seixas, the Warden of the congregation wrote to Washington, praising him and this new nation that "to bigotry is gives no sanction."[14] Seixas continued,

> Deprived as we heretofore have been of the invaluable rights of free Citizens, we now with a deep sense of gratitude to the Almighty disposer of all events behold a Government, erected by the Majesty of the People -- a Government, which to bigotry gives no sanction, to persecution no assistance -- but generously affording to all Liberty of conscience, and immunities of Citizenship: deeming every one, of whatever Nation, tongue, or language equal parts of the great governmental Machine."

Washington responded to the congregation, supporting the idea of the First Amendment and the need for religious tolerance. He said in part,

> The Citizens of the United States of America have a right to applaud themselves for having given to mankind examples of an enlarged and liberal policy: a policy worthy of imitation. All possess a like liberty of

conscience and immunities of citizenship. It is now no more that toleration is spoken of, as if it was by the indulgence of one class of people, that another enjoyed the exercise of their inherent natural rights. For happily the Government of the United States, which gives to bigotry no sanction, to persecution no assistance requires only that they who live under its protection should demean themselves as good citizens, in giving it on all occasions their effectual support. [15]

Washington's response was not in support of a Christian nation, as some Christian nation proponents believe, but the acceptance of a Jewish congregation into the folds of the new nation without prejudice. Washington's letter made no mention of religion.

Jews were, and still are, the one of most persecuted religious people on the planet. Even before the Spanish Inquisition, Rome scattered Jews throughout their empire as merchants, government intermediaries, and to break up the Jewish rebellions. Washington and other Founders knew this well and the acceptance of Touro Synagogue as an American religious institution only serve to strengthen the Constitution and William's dream.

༺༻

The Heathens of Ma-re Mount

Ma-re Mount, its name a pun for the Latin word "mare" meaning sea, was the second Massachusetts settlement, founded in 1624 by lawyer Thomas Morton.[16] Morton was what we would call today a Secular Humanist and Pagan, wanting his settlement to return to the old English Pagan ways which included the celebration of May Day, complete with dance, drink, and the erection of and dancing around a Maypole. If that was not enough to infuriate his overly and overtly intolerant neighbors to the south, Morton invited the Algonquin natives to join the affair so Ma-re Mount men could marry Algonquin women. This absolute tolerance, belief in full integration and their intellectual thought infuriated the puritans of Plymouth to the point of attacking the Ma-re Mount settlement.

Massachusetts Governor William Bradford attacked and overtook the settlement without a shot, destroying the settlement and disbanding the settlers. Morton was sent back to England where he continued his fight against puritan and protestant religious and secular intolerance.[17]

Ma-re Mount may have been short in longevity and its existence muted, but the knowledge that a group of English pagans even attempted to create a New World settlement is a revelation to many and apparently a fact simply ignored by the proponents of the Christian nation position.

The Other Colonies

The other 12 colonies had "state" religions dependent upon and supported by law and by tax, and they remained mostly intolerant to other sects of Christianity and non-Christian beliefs. However, only Massachusetts can be deemed as a colony based on religion, and even then only somewhat. The Carolinas were founded as trade colonies for tobacco, cotton, and lumber.

Though Georgia was not established until 1734, its purpose was to establish trade and create an alternative to the British debtor prisons, as well as a barrier of protection from Spanish, French, and the original settlers of the region, the American Indians.[18]

The New World settlements did provide a safe haven for many of the new breakaway and persecuted religions, Pennsylvania for the Quakers and Maryland for British Catholics. Like Rhode Island, William Penn declared religious tolerance and freedom early in the establishment of the colony that bore his name.

Yes, William Penn was a devout Quaker; however, Pennsylvania had commerce as its primary role.

In 1682, Penn declared that "All men have a natural and indefeasible right to worship Almighty God according to the dictates of their own consciences; no man can of right be compelled to attend, erect, or support any place of worship… against his consent."[19] Penn's belief was that his new colony was not to be established to only protect members of the Society of Friends but to allow all people of all beliefs a safe haven.

Sweden even had its New World settlement near the modern day city of Williams Port, Maryland. Sweden was considered a world power in the late 1500s and early 1600s in commerce and in exploration, so creating a new settlement in the newly discovered territory was a natural fit.

As a purely business venture, Swedish, Dutch and German investors founded the settlement of New Sweden in 1638, establishing a beachhead for fur and tobacco trade.[20] The colony would eventually extend itself along and control most of the Delaware River.

The Dutch also had claims along the Delaware. When the governor of New Sweden allowed the Dutch to build a fort in its territory in 1654, the governor of New Amsterdam, Peter Stuyvesant, sent war ships and a small contingent of about 320 men to take the territory. They did and the land came under Dutch control.

From the mouth of the Delaware River north to its major city, New Amsterdam, onward to what is now Albany, and including most of Long Island and the entire Hudson Valley, the Dutch East Indian Company established the settlement of New Amsterdam in 1624, not to spread Christianity but, again, for the commerce.[21]

New Amsterdam, renamed New York City after the British took control, remained a key port and an extremely religiously diverse city from its original colonization. Holland's New World tolerance was famous, with reports of Huguenots, Quakers, Presbyterians, Roman Catholics, even, according to one contemporary essayist, "many atheists and various other servants of Baal."[22] Today New York City remains one of the most secular and religiously diverse cities in the world.

As early as "1654, the *Sainte Catherine* pulled into port of New Amsterdam carrying 23 Sephardic Jews, refugees from Recifé Spain. Why did they choose New Amsterdam? The Netherlands was the most religiously tolerant society in Europe in the 17th century and that tradition of tolerance marked New Amsterdam as well."[23]

༺༻

On The Other Side...

When discussing the American experiment, one must remember that the British, French and Dutch were not the only colonists of the New World. It is wrong to forget about the other major exploiters of the new land, the Spanish, and the minor player, France.

On the other side of the continent, well before the founding of Jamestown, the Spanish were already seeking gold, spices and a way to the Orient. Their primary goal was to plunder the riches of the new land, returning them to the Spanish crown. Monks followed along to monitor the spiritual needs of the conquistadors and to spread the word of Christ to the heathens. If one did not convert, torture and death soon followed. As the monks evangelized to the original Americans, the same rules of the Tribunal of the Holy Office of the Inquisition (*Tribunal del Santo Oficio de la Inquisición*) and the Spanish Inquisition (*Inquisición española*), as established by King Ferdinand and Queen Isabella and approved by Pope Sixtus IV in 1478, applied.[24] Change or die.

The Spanish founded Santa Fe as the capital of Nuevo Mexico in 1607, not with the goal to spread the Gospel, but as a base of government, military, and trade. The Spanish mission was a place to rest and eat after travel or battle, more so than as it was a place of worship. All of the monasteries found along the California coast, New Mexico and Arizona, were as much stops for weary travelers, traders, and conquistadors as they were churches. Many were centers of commerce for wine producers, bakeries, and local farms, and were sites of local secular meetings and government.

Santa Fe remains the oldest capital city in the United States as the capital of New Mexico while retaining much of its Spanish heritage.

America's oldest city, St. Augustine, Florida (established in 1565) also has a rich nonsectarian history. Initially the site was discovered by Spanish explorer Ponce de Leon who, as the stories go, was searching for the fountain of youth. Eventually, Juan Menendez de Aviles established the city where it sits today, as the center of Spanish military and commerce in the Floridas. The original rationale for the city was not religious but military; the need to counter the opening of a French fort in the Caribbean threatening Spanish commerce. Religion was not in the primary picture.

ಙ೫ಲ೫ಲಙ

Conclusion

If by "Founding" one would mean the initial colonization of the New World, the primary reason for the establishments of the colonies, including Massachusetts, was for commerce, not Christian expansion. This is not a misconception or a misreading of history, but is based on the documents available. The notion that Christianity was the primary reason for settlement or possibly the secondary reason is itself the misreading of history by those who wish otherwise. It is historical fact that can be verified in documents that few, unfortunately, have read in their entirety.

Many did immigrate to the New World to escape religious persecution and some of those wanted to establish religious communities based on their sect's beliefs. However, these appear to be limited to settlements and not entire colonies, nor the reason for the various European strongholds to establish footholds in the Americas.

The majority of immigrants to the new country were European; therefore, it is only natural that Christianity would be the majority religion in America and Canada. In addition, the original charters were mainly English, thus establishing the language and protestant churches, especially the Anglican Church, in the colonies. Yet, as we have seen, many other religions were represented in the New World well before 1763, a time when many historians believe the first seeds of the Revolution were planted.

However, if "founding" means the years leading to the signing of the Constitution of the United States of America, separate proofs need to be discussed.

Chapter 6

THE GUYS IN WIGS

One correspondent declared that he could provide "real objective evidence" that the United States government was founded on Judeo-Christian principles. The writer said, "Look who the Founding Fathers were. They all believed in Judeo-Christian values of justice and freedom. There were no Muslims or Buddhists among them." And she is right. Of the 204 men and women who are today considered "Founders," there were no Muslims or Buddhists among them, also no Jews, no Baptists, and no Evangelicals. Of the 55 men who signed the Constitution, most were Episcopalian/Anglicans or Presbyterians.

> Sidebar - Today many Jews will argue that there really is no such thing as Judeo-Christian principles.[1] There are the laws given to the Jews by God in the Torah and the principles given to the people by Jesus in his Sermon on the Mount. Some Jews are, in fact, insulted by the phrase, believing that it somehow aligns the Jewish beliefs with the Christian beliefs when 1) the Christians used and changed

the Torah as the beginning of their Bible, and 2) there is no connection between the Jewish Messiah and Jesus.

Muslims are also quick to point out that the Qur'an refers to both the Torah and to the prophet Jesus. Islam's belief system includes many of the stories from the Torah and uses the teachings of Christian Bible as a basis for many of the Prophet's teachings.

The Founders were well aware of what religion had done to the British government. Europe, with the possible single exception of Holland, was ruled by theocratic-monarchies. The Founders were theists, deists and maybe a closet atheist or two, but agreed on one thing; the imposition of a national religion would only lead to the same governmental horrors they had seen and lived within Europe and as the colonies of England.

However, in the 1750s there were Muslims, Jews and Catholics living in the American colonies and they were discriminated against, as were all other minority religions and races. Does this justify the claim that because the signers of the Constitution were all white, European men, and most of who belonged formally to a Christian discipline, that the United States is a Christian nation? Far from it. It only proves that European white Christian men were the dominant force in American politics at the time, as they are today.

Minorities of religion or race, as well as women, were not of the "privileged class" and, therefore, not part of the "creation" of this new nation and government. As the adage says, "Those who rule write the history," and the laws.

Many of the men who assisted in writing the Declaration of Independence and the Constitution, and those who participated in the various state ratification conventions were believers in a supreme power, a creator of the universe or a personal God. Fifty-four percent were associated with the Anglican Church alone, but not all considered themselves Christians.[2] I say "not all" because the religious affiliation of a person did not necessarily agree with that person's practices. As today, many went to their church to avoid the social ramifications.

This chapter is not meant as an in depth biography of each of our Founders. Others have done a much better job than I. However, these are short summaries concerning the religious affiliation, practice and the influence religion had on each.

The Deists

Jefferson and Franklin were Deists, believing not in a god who watches over and guides individuals through their daily lives, but in "the Laws of Nature and of Nature's God." Today this is known as Natural Science, something with which men of the 18th Century Enlightenment were very familiar. Nature's God was not the God of Abraham but something larger and greater, something, as Einstein would later suggest, that was greater than man's imagination could conceive.

Deism is a misunderstood realm of religion with some believing it is another sect of Christianity. Deism is not a "revealed" religion as are Christianity, Judaism and Islam. The "truth" to the deist is based on nature, nature's laws, and on reason. Depending on the individual, some may say "God-given reason." But this god does not fit the same ideal of the Jewish, Muslim or Christian Supreme Being. It refers to a universal unifying force that gave the laws of nature and the laws of reason.

Some deists believed that God created the world, some do not. Most deists follow the philosophy of *Ex nusquam, panton;* "from nothing, everything." Some believed in original sin, but most do not. What holds the deist apart from other Western faiths is that deists do not believe in mysticism but in reason. The proof of the deity is not revealed but can be found in nature's laws and that those laws cannot be broken, not even by the God of Abraham.

Deists are not anti-religion and are not atheists. Unlike the atheistic "there is no god", deists believe there is a supreme power, a "god" per se, but that god is undefined and the laws of that god are discovered through intellect, not through revelation.

Deists, like Jefferson, did not and do not see a direct relationship between man's laws and biblical law. To the deist, unlike some of their Christian, Jewish and Islamic counterparts, politics and religion are like water and oil; they simply just do not mix.

One must also understand the meaning of the language as used in the second half of the 1700s and by the deists of the time.[3] Deists, then and now, do not believe in the Trinity or in a personal god. Jefferson did believe that there was a creator, not a Christian or Jewish God, but something greater. Deists call this idea "The Creator," "Providence," "Author of our Being," and "Nature's God," thus the language we find in the Virginia Act of Religious Freedom and the Declaration of Independence. It can be argued that Nature is the true supreme being, to which God bowed.

One of the unsung influences in American constitutional history may be the Religious Society of Friends – the Quakers. As one of the many "nonconformist" religions in Europe, its American roots come from seeking a better life without prejudice. Their unorthodox form of Christianity can be summarized in John 1:9 (KJV), "If we confess our sins, he is faithful and just to forgive us our sins, and to cleanse us from all unrighteousness."

It is the mistaken relationship between faith, religion, and association with personal practices and politics that is of issue. Here are some examples of belief versus affiliation versus participation of our

Founders.

☙❧

Thomas Jefferson was raised in an Anglican home, one of ten siblings. Though not devout as a boy, he knew his bible lessons well. It was when he left home for college that he discovered the French and Scottish enlightenments and the art of critical thinking.

He crossed from Anglican to atheist to deist over the coming years.[4] There are stories that Jefferson attended church after his leaving public office, and for the most part, these are true. However, Jefferson did not relish one sect over any other and never took communion in the Anglican Church.

Jefferson's belief in a pluralistic society was so strong that he authored and lobbied to pass the *Virginia Act for Establishing Religious Freedom*.[5] The Act was initially introduced in 1779 but it took seven years until passage with the help of Jefferson's good friend and fellow Virginian, James Madison.

Jefferson's belief in the pluralism of government was clear and well documented. This Founder also believed that his writing of the Virginia Act was more important than his writing of the Declaration of Independence.

"It is in our lives," Jefferson would later write, "and not our words that religion must be read."[6]

In 1804, Jefferson took the King James Version of the New Testament and, with scissors and paste, removed those things that made no sense to him or did not fit with "the Laws of Nature," and put the bible back together. Gone were the virgin birth and many of the miracles that appeared to Jefferson to have no basis because even Nature's God would not violate Nature's Laws.

Jefferson did not call his work by today's common name, "The

Jefferson Bible," but *The life and morals of Jesus of Nazareth extracted textually from the Gospels*.[7] There are a multiple of editions of the *Jefferson Bible* on the market; however, the best will show some of the original Jefferson papers as he worked on this project and portions of the cut-and-paste itself.

For those brave enough to get this far, I ask that you read the *The life and morals of Jesus of Nazareth extracted textually from the Gospels*. Regardless of your faith or non-faith, this is a wonderful place to find a deist's vision of religion, God and Nature.

In 1801, the congregation of the Danbury Baptist Association was very concerned about the new government and, considering the extreme politicalization of religion during the election of 1800, wanted President Jefferson to reaffirm his position on religious freedom and the First Amendment to the Constitution. They wished that such religious freedoms would be extended by the individual states.

> Sir, we are sensible that the president of the United States is not the national legislator, and also sensible that the national government cannot destroy the laws of each state; but our hopes are strong that the sentiments of our beloved president, which have had such genial effect already, like the radiant beams of the sun, will shine and prevail through all these states and all the world, till hierarchy and tyranny be destroyed from the earth.[8]

In his 1802 response to the Danbury Baptist Association concerning the "Establishment Clause" of the First Amendment, Jefferson wrote,

> Believing with you that religion is a matter which lies solely between Man & his God, that he owes account to none other for his faith or his worship, that the

> legitimate powers of government reach actions only, & not opinions, I contemplate with sovereign reverence that act of the whole American people which declared that their legislature should "make no law respecting an establishment of religion, or prohibiting the free exercise thereof," thus *building a wall of separation between Church & State.* Adhering to this expression of the supreme will of the nation in behalf of the rights of conscience, I shall see with sincere satisfaction the progress of those sentiments which tend to restore to man all his natural rights, convinced he has no natural right in opposition to his social duties. (Italics added)[9]

There is a section of this letter that was removed from the final draft sent to Danbury that provides further insight as to Jefferson's beliefs in the prohibiting a national or state religion.

> Congress thus inhibited from acts respecting religion, and the Executive authorized only to execute their acts, I have refrained from prescribing even those occasional perform-ances of devotion, practiced indeed by the Executive of another nation [England] as the legal head of its church, but subject here, as religious exercises only to the voluntary regulations and discipline of each respective sect.[10]

He closed his letter acknowledging the faith of those of the Danbury Baptist Association and his own conscience. "I reciprocate your kind prayers for the protection & blessing of the common father and creator of man, and tender you for yourselves & your religious association, assurances of my high respect & esteem."

The "wall" may be a bad metaphor today, but Jefferson's position was clear and based upon the history of England and the colonies; that marriage of church and state had been and would continue to be disastrous to the citizenry.

To say that Jefferson was some sort of radical and not typical among his peers would be an incorrect statement. Even those of religious fervor such as James Madison, John Adams, and others can be defined by their personal religious practices, at least in part, as deists. The confusion here is differentiating between affiliation and practice, between faith in the supernatural and faith in reason.

Did Jefferson "walk away" from the Christian faith? It depends on whether the questioner believes that Jefferson was ever a Christian. He was brought up in the Anglican Church but never baptized. He rarely went to church, but when he did, Jefferson did not favor one sect or denomin-ation over another. He gave money to help build a Catholic church and established a great secular university.

⋅⋅⋅⋅⋅⋅

Benjamin Franklin's religion was eclectic and a many today get it wrong. Franklin was born in Massachusetts of a puritan family, he was not a Quaker as some may believe. There is truth in the fact that Franklyn was not a practicing puritan - or just did not comply by the faith's strict rules of behavior.

At 16, Franklin resettled in Philadelphia where he was free of the puritan church and its rules. Philadelphia was quite cosmopolitan and Franklin found, as a printer, his way into the intellectual life of the city.

Franklin was most likely a deist, having taken a different view of God than the mainstream puritans of Boston; he did not accept the concept of the Trinity.

Franklin, like many other Founders, read the Bible as well as Crane Briton's contribution to the *Encyclopedia of Philosophy,* John Locke's *Two Treaties on Government,* and Aristotle's *Republic* and *Ethics*.[11]

Many deists referred to Briton's works as the *Book of Nature*. This is a primary reason Jefferson, Franklin and other deists referred to "Laws of Nature and of Nature's God."

Some suggest that Franklin was a polytheist, one who believed in many gods. Some of his writings suggest that Franklin believed in a "Creator" (deist) as well as individual gods who were charged with each solar system in the universe, as evidenced in his letters as the Ambassador to France. However, men occasionally change their minds.

In 1787, during the debates concerning the ratification of the new Constitution, Franklin gave a passionate speech concerning God and the limited powers of man, "the imperfection of Human Understanding."[12] The 81-year old Franklin saw that the great impasse within the Pennsylvania convention needed something to move it forward towards ratification. In that, Franklin asked that the convention open its sessions with a formal prayer. In part, he told the assembly,

> ...the longer I live, the more convincing proofs I see of this Truth--that God governs in the Affairs of Men... I also believe without his concurring Aid, we shall succeed in this political Building no better than the Builders of Babel.
>
> I therefore beg leave to move – that henceforth prayers imploring the assistance of Heaven, and its blessings on our deliberations, be held in this Assembly every morning before we proceed to business, and that one or more of the Clergy of this City (Philadelphia) be requested to officiate in that Service.[13]

The motion was seconded, debated, and then permanently postponed by the assembly. It died a quiet death simply for the lack of funding to pay the minister, as well as a lack of interest.

However, Franklin never supported a national religion and supported the call for a secular nation.

☙❧

George Washington rarely went to church and rarely referred to God or Jesus in his correspondence, contrary to what some may suggest. Washington held his beliefs to himself and appeared more of a military man than anything else. Unfortunately, this never stopped various religious organizations from claiming Washington as one of their own.

Washington was a member of the Episcopal Church, though rarely attended services. There is a story, though not verified as many of the myths about the "father of our country," that a minister of the church once asked Washington to leave after the General fell asleep during services once too often. The story continues that Washington would drop Martha off at services and leave to conduct the nation's business.

Thomas Kidd, in his *God of Liberty – A religious history of the American Revolution*, suggests that General Washington used the ministry for the morale (not moral) value and encouragement "assuring the [Continental Army] that God was on their side."[14] This is verified in a number of other Washington biographies and studies.

One must remember that most of the people in the new nation were illiterate and the majority of their information did not come from the hundreds of pamphlets and newspapers, but from the pulpit of the local church. The use of the local churches to spread the word of the Revolution would, therefore, be understandable though secular in nature.

However, the notion that Washington invoked God in all general orders while in command of the Continental Army is simply not correct. His use of language and any reference to God, much like that of patriot

Samuel Adams as we shall see later, was more to create a secular moral code, of conduct for the officers of the Army using what the volunteers knew best, the Bible.

Washington never moved from his belief in the new nation's and the Constitution's pluralistic nature. In one of the few statements Washington made concerning religion and the Constitution, he responded to a query made by the United Baptist Churches of Virginia. The church wrote,

> "But amidst all the inquietudes of mind, our consolation arose from this consideration, the plan must be good, for it bears the signature of a tried, trusty friend; and if religious liberty is rather insecure in the constitution the administration will certainly prevent all oppression, for a WASHINGTON will preside.[15]"

The problem brought forth by the Baptists was the lack of any law concerning the right to religious practice and the prohibition of a nationalized faith. Their letter, sent two years prior to the 1791 adoption of the Bill of Rights, was of deep concern for religious freedom for them and many other "secondary" Protestant sects as well as the Catholics and Jews now living in the new nation.

Washington's May 10, 1789 response to the church was unequivocal - religious freedoms would prosper under his administration. Many quote only the last sentence of his letter, which states Washington's sentiment, but here is the entire paragraph.

> If I could have entertained the slightest apprehension that the Constitution framed in the Convention, where I had the honor to preside, might possibly endanger the religious rights of any ecclesiastical society, certainly I would never have placed my signature to it; and if I could now conceive that the general government might

> ever be so administered as to render the liberty of conscience insecure, I beg you will be persuaded that no one would be more zealous than myself to establish effectual barriers against the horrors of spiritual tyranny, and every species of religious persecution. For you, doubtless, remember that I have often expressed my sentiment, that every man, conducting himself as a good citizen, and being accountable to God alone for his religious opinions, ought to be protected in worshipping the Deity according to the dictates of his own conscience.[16]

Though Washington did not refer to the document directly, he was greatly influenced by Jefferson's "Virginia Act for Religious Freedom." Passed in 1786, but prior to the adoption of the First Amendment, it was Washington's comments to a Jewish congregation, not Christian, that helped solidify a national consensus of religious tolerance.

In 1790, President Washington responded to a letter from the Hebrew Congregation of Newport, Rhode Island. As with the Baptists, the Jewish community was concerned about religious tolerance under the new national constitution and government. Washington responded to their concerns,

> The citizens of the United States of America have a right to applaud themselves for having given to mankind examples of an enlarged and liberal policy-a policy worthy of imitation. All possess alike liberty of conscience and immunities of citizenship.

> It is now no more that toleration is spoken as if it were the indulgence of one class of people that another enjoy the exercise of their inherent natural rights, for, happily, the Government of the United States, which gives to

bigotry no sanction, to persecution no assistance, requires only that they who live under its protection should demean themselves as good citizens in giving it on all occasions their effectual support.

There is no reference to God or the Christian faith in either of these responses, or many others. There is, however, a clear indication that Washington was more aligned as a deist and that he saw religious freedom essential for the survival of the new nation.

The Washington Myths

Preacher Mason Weems created most of the stories relating to Washington as a religious man and the myths we learn in school.[17] Weems' contention was something we have seen before and since; that such a great man as Washington could not exist without the help of God, so the history of the man known as the "Father of our country" was tweaked. A lot.

It was Weems who also gave us the Washington who knelt in prayer at Valley Forge, Washington chopping down of the cherry tree, and Washington throwing a silver dollar across the Potomac River. There is no historic verification of the first two and unless the President was at the headwaters of the river or Superman, it is not possible to accomplish such a feat of strength as throwing anything across that divide near Mount Vernon.

❈❈❈

Patrick Henry was a man of many occupations but a master of none until he entered law and politics. He was also a devout Anglican who would change his position on the separation issue a few times.

Henry, as you may recall, was the member of the Virginia constitutional convention who said, "Give me liberty or... give me death" in his famed, but seldom read, 1775 speech.[†] However, he was also an early defender of religious freedoms.

For Henry, politics and religion were brothers within the same family. His father, John Henry, was the appointed judge for Western Virginia and his uncle, the Reverend Patrick Henry, stood in the pulpit of the St. Paul Anglican Church. However, there is very little written about the younger Henry's upbringing and religious education. We are fairly certain that he did not wish to follow his uncle to the pulpit.

We do know that his first real success came in the form of a legal argument against the Church of England and for the recognition of the other religions in the colony of Virginia.

Most of the quotes attributed to Henry concerning his religion and his belief that there should be a recognized state church are taken from his later years, when Henry was aligned with Alexander Hamilton in seeking a national religion as a Federalist. As with his childhood, there are few quotes concerning his religion or beliefs before a faithful day in 1763.

Henry's attempts as a farmer, a merchant, and a tavern owner all failed. His father finally encouraged Henry to take up law. He eventually passed the bar, but the shy and soft spoken Henry never litigated a case, but acted as a "paper attorney," one dealing in contract and wills. That is until he was approach by the Western Virginia Baptist Association.

What most do not know is that Henry's rhetorical skills were considered some of the finest in the colonies. Those skills were honed in the courtroom, beginning with this single and his first court case.

In Virginia, the Church of England was fully supported by the taxes

---

[†] See "Referenced Documents" for Henry's complete address.

collected by the colony and, because currency was scarce, payment was accepted in the form of tobacco, the prime crop of the region -- 16,000 pounds of tobacco per parish. The parsons then sold the tobacco at "two pence per pound."[18] However, Virginia had suffered a drought that caused many a farmer to go bankrupt and many parsonages received less than their 16,000 pounds allotment. In addition, the demands for tobacco were increasing both in the colonies and in Europe and, as students of economics know, when supply dwindles and demand enlarges, the price goes up.

To make matters more interesting, the Two Penny Act of Virginia allowed the parsons to be paid in cash. That would have averaged to approximately V£ 130 (Virginia Pounds), which the landowners paid. Yet with the increased prices, the ministers believed that they would have made V£ 400 and sued for the difference. The Presbyterians, Baptists and other non-Anglican Christians and non-Christians refused to pay because the Church of England was not their church.

The Church's argument was that the citizens, all citizens, must support the Church as stated in Isaiah 49:23. (KJV)

> And kings shall be thy nursing fathers, and their queens thy nursing mothers: they shall bow down to thee with their face toward the earth, and lick up the dust of thy feet; and thou shalt know that I am the LORD: for they shall not be ashamed that wait for me.

So on December 1, 1763, Patrick Henry stood in a courtroom about to give the first of many penetrating speeches of his life.

Henry's argument was simple. The Anglican Church did not represent the Baptist families in western Virginia and, in Henry's words,

> ...snatched from the hearth of their honest parishioner

his last hoe-cake [a cornmeal flatbread], from the widow and her orphaned children their last milchcow [milk cow]! The last bed, nay, the last blanket from the lay-in woman!

He argued that the farmers, landowners and artisans of Virginia had the right to keep what they earned and that the Church had no right to take those earnings from them. His anger against the Church and its seizure of political power in Virginia was so powerful that Henry's speech "chased" many Anglican ministers from the courthouse.[19] We know his esteemed uncle was in the courtroom. We do not know if he stayed.

His secondary argument was that church and state were not equal partners in government and that the direct support of any church by the government was wrong. Henry may not have been the first to cry foul, but he was certainly the best and at the time, the loudest.

Henry won his case and became a major voice of the Revolution.

Henry lit one of the first of many fuses of revolutionary dissent in the colonies. First was the right of every freeman to be protected from undue taxes without proper representation. Later in life, as we shall read, Henry switched teams.

John Adams wrote, "I never write or talk about divinity. I have had more than I could do of humanity."

Adams was a Unitarian and "rejected many fundamental doctrines of conventional Christianity, such as the Trinity and the divinity of Jesus."[20] Paul C. Nagel is quoted in *The Faiths of our Fathers* as saying that Adams' philosophy was shaped by his puritan and Calvinist background, or at least their settings.[21]

What Adams did know was the atrocities formulated by a nationally sanctioned church, such as the Church of England. In the colonies of the 18 Century, the power of the Church was indeed greater than the civil government.

From various biographies and descriptions of Adams, he too could be called a deist though he retained is Unitarian affiliation and attended church regularly when in Massachusetts. He would also use his Unitarian faith as a weapon in the presidential election of 1800.

Adams talked and wrote little about his own beliefs, but he and Abigail took time to go to church when he visited his home in Bainbridge. Because of his deep deistic-leaning belief in a "Creator," Adams considered his relationship with the God of Nature in most decisions. Yet, the Bible was not his only reference to the divine, for Greek, Roman, and Hebrew writings would add to his knowledge of faith. Finally, many biographers tell stories of Adams' continual feeling of remorse due to his vanity, his anger, his distrust, and his paranoia of others that he always felt guilty in the eyes of his God.[22]

Adams was as much a pious man as he was a defender of religious freedom and it was on that basis that his friendship with Jefferson began, would later break and come together again. As with many of the more religious founders, Adams understood there more faiths than Christianity represented in the new land. Boston alone saw various Christian sects, Jews, non-believers and Muslims who visited the city during their treks across the Atlantic.

Adams worked with Jefferson on the Declaration of Independence and had the foresight to see the error in the New England political position of the combining of the religious and political worlds.

In 2005, political activist Roy Herron of Tennessee and a 2010 U.S. Congressional candidate wrote, *God and Politics: How a Christian Can Be In Politics*.[23] In his introduction, Herron provides yet another "proof" that Adams believed that faith and patriotism were one and the same, thus supporting the Christian nation position. He wrote, "In 1775, John Adams wrote his wife, Abigail, 'Statesmen may plan and speculate for Liberty, but it is Religion and Morality alone which can establish the principles upon which Freedom can securely stand.' Adams believed that 'a Patriot must be a religious man.'"

However, this is more than likely incorrect. In his book *Founding Faiths*, Steven Waldman wrote in the postscript notes:

> Conservatives have misquoted (John) Adams as well. M. Stanton Evans in *The American Spectator*, February, 2007, quoted Adams as saying, "Statesmen may plan and speculate for liberty, but its Religion and Morality which establish the principles upon which freedom can securely stand. A Patriot must be a religious man.
>
> "Who would not Exchange the discordant Scenes of Envy, Pride, Vanity, Malice, Revenge, for the sweet Consolations of Philosophy, the serene Composure of the Passions, the divine Enjoyments of Christian Charity, and Benevolence?
>
> "Statesmen my dear Sire, may plan and speculate for Liberty, but it is Religion and Morality alone, which can establish the Principles upon which Freedom can securely stand...
>
> The only foundation of a free Constitution is pure virtue, and if this cannot be inspired into our People, in a greater Measure, than they have it now. They may change their Rulers, and forms of Government, but they will not obtain a lasting Liberty." [24]

Waldman continued by stating that in his research Adams did not write, "A patriot must be a religious man." However, his wife Abigail did write, "A patriot without religion, in my estimation, is as great a paradox as an honest man without the fear of God," in a letter to her friend Mercy Warren on November 5, 1775.[25] His proofs appear to have stronger citations than Herron's.

During the research for this book, there was no substantiation of Walden's claims; however, there are numerous references to Abigail's letters. In other words, the words of John and Abigail Adams were possibly rearranged to meet Mr. Herron's collective religious and political goals. Or, as with others, he was given this quote as "the truth" and never followed up to verify the statement.

There is also a possible case of literary liberty in argument that is much like the Finagle Factor: add, subtract, multiply or divide by any number to your formula to make the answer right. In terms of quotations; add, misrepresentation, rearrange or invent. Or all of the above.

೫೩೮೦೮೦೮೩

James Madison, our fourth president, was an Episcopalian who attended St. John's Church in Virginia regularly.[26] His religious beliefs are not be questioned, for he was a pious man. It was his belief that service to God in the temporal world could not be better served than by enjoying the fruits of one's labor, that belief as a Christian will bring prosperity. Mapp quotes Madison as saying:

> I have sometimes thought there could not be a stronger testimony in favor of Religion against Temporal enjoyments even the most rational and manly than for men who occupy the most honorable and gainful departments and are rising in reputation and wealth, publicly to declare their unsatisfactories by becoming fervent advocate in the cause of Christ, and I wish you

may give your evidence in this way.[27]

Yet it was he and Thomas Jefferson who rallied for religious freedom in the Commonwealth of Virginia. And it was in Virginia where politics and religion came to one if its first battles in the life of the new nation. Madison called for the removal of the Anglican Church as the official church of Virginia, opposing any continued collection of taxes to support the church along with Patrick Henry.

It was Madison's small size, five-foot one-inch, and possible epilepsy that caused him to shy from public speaking. Yet during the debate concerning Jefferson's proposed bill, Madison spoke with a passion, as great if not greater than Patrick Henry, exalting that the proposed legislation would "disestablished" the Episcopal Church and force them to live like all other churches in Virginia, without tax support.[28]

It was in February of 1788 when the master of words became the master of the pen. In the Federalist Papers number 51 and 56, Madison glorified the new Constitution's Article VI's declaration that "no religious Test shall ever be required as a Qualification to any Office or public Trust under the United States." Madison would later write, "The door of the Federal Government is open to merit of every description, whether native or adoptive, whether young or old, without regard to poverty or wealth, or to any particular profession of religious faith."

His position on the distinction between secular and sectarian law was undeniable.[29] In an 1823 letter, Madison wrote, "Religion is essentially distinct from civil government and exempt from cognizance... a connection between them in injurious to both."[30] Madison's position, as Jefferson's, was so strong that he introduced and fought for Jefferson's Virginia Act for Religious Freedom though its final passage.

As President of the United States, he opposed the incorporation of the Protestant Episcopal Church in Washington, D.C., stating that to do such would set a "dangerous union of civil and religious authority."[31]

Sometime after his second term as President, Madison wrote "Monopolies Perpetuities Corporations Ecclesiastical Endowments."[32] In this undated "memorandum," Madison spoke to a number of issues and his justifications for decisions made during his presidency. As the title suggests, this manuscript discusses two important issues. The first, the "monopolies," concerns copyrights and patents. Madison reminded his reader, "The Constitution of the U. S. has limited them to two cases, the authors of Books, and of useful inventions, in both which they are considered as a compensation for a benefit actually gained to the community as a purchase of property which the owner might otherwise withhold from public use."

It is the second discussion that attracts attention. Madison begins the discussion with a direct and bold statement. "The danger of silent accumulations & encroachments by Ecclesiastical Bodies have not sufficiently engaged attention in the U. S."

Madison continued his argument with a very familiar refrain,

> Ye States of America, which retain in your Constitutions or Codes, any aberration from the sacred principle of religious liberty, by giving to Caesar what belongs to God, or joining together what God has put asunder, hasten to revise & purify your systems, and make the example of your Country as pure & compleat, in what relates to the freedom of the mind and its allegiance to its maker, as in what belongs to the legitimate objects of political & civil institutions.

Madison's reference to Matthew 22 is direct and made as a warning to those governing the country. It is here where the strongest evidence that the United States Constitution was not based on a biblical code and the government was, as Lincoln would say two-score years later, "of the people, by the people, for the people," but not of any church.

If Madison were alive today, he would have a great deal to say concerning the issue of America as a Christian nation. Most likely, as hypothesized from his writings and actions, Madison would deny any connection whatsoever.

Certainly Madison would have a few words to say concerning today's "Awakening," as he did in an 1822 letter to Edward Livingston where he said,

> Nothwithstanding the general progress made within the two last centuries in favour of this branch of liberty, & the full establishment of it, in some parts of our Country, there remains in others a strong bias towards the old error, that without some sort of alliance or coalition between Gov' & Religion neither can be duly supported: Such indeed is the tendency to such a coalition, and such its corrupting influence on both the parties, that the danger cannot be too carefully guarded agst...

☙❧❧☙

Thomas Paine, author of *Common Sense*, which Washington reportedly had read to his troops at Valley Forge, was not a Christian, but a deist, possibly agnostic, who stood firmly to the concept of a pluralistic society with no state religion. [33] In his chapter "Thoughts on the Present state of American Affairs" Paine noted the increasing immigration from the entire continent of Europe and wrote, "This new world hath been the asylum for persecuted lovers of civil and religious liberty from every part of Europe." [34]

He continued,

> Yet that we do not appear defective in earthly honors, let a day be solemnly set apart for proclaiming the charter (of the new nation); let it be brought forth on divine law, the word of God; let the crown be placed thereon, by which the world would know, that so far as we approve of monarchy, that in America THE LAW IS KING. (Original capitalization retained)

And those laws were to be made by man and were to be honored by man. For the new nation, those laws began with the Continental Congress, moving in 1776 to the Confederation of the United States, and finally rewritten in 1787 in to the embodiment of our present day Constitution of the United States.

Thomas' own religious beliefs were not hidden from the public. In *The Age of Reason*, written in 1794, Paine said,

> I believe in one God, and no more; and I hope for happiness beyond this life. I believe in the equality of man; and I believe that religious duties consist in doing justice, loving mercy, and endeavoring to make our fellow-creatures happy.
>
> But, lest it should be supposed that I believe in many other things in addition to these, I shall, in the progress of this work, declare the things I do not believe, and my reasons for not believing them.
>
> I do not believe in the creed professed by the Jewish Church, by the Roman Church, by the Greek Church, by the Turkish Church, by the Protestant Church, nor by any Church that I know of. My own mind is my own Church."[35]

It was within *The Age of Reason* that Paine best described his disdain for religion of any manner.

> All national institutions of churches, whether Jewish, Christian or Turkish [Muslim], appear to me no other than human inventions, set up to terrify and enslave mankind, and monopolize power and profit.
>
> I do not mean by this declaration to condemn those who believe otherwise; they have the same right to their belief as I have to mine. But it is necessary to the happiness of man, that he be mentally faithful to himself. Infidelity does not consist in believing, or in disbelieving; it consists in professing to believe what he does not believe.[36]

To say that Paine was simply a radical kook ala Jefferson would be to understate his influence on the American experiment. As a pamphleteer and printer, he had a special relationship with the American people. *Common Sense* and *Age of Reason* were widely distributed and read. Today, Americans continue underestimate the value and power of both documents.

ଓଛୋଚଓ

Alexander Hamilton argued with passion for a federally recognized and tax supported religion, but those occurred mostly during the elections of 1800 and the arguments fell on deaf ears.

Yet, Hamilton was one of the most irreligious of all of the founders; a drinker, womanizer, and money lender who would never back down from an insult real or imaginary. Today, Hamilton, a High Federalist, the founder of the Bank of the U.S., and ardent defender of the federal rights above all others, is seen with both praise and suspicion by many.

During the 1787 Virginia Constitutional Convention, Hamilton said, "For my own part, I sincerely esteem [the Constitution as] a system which, without the finger of God, never could have been suggested and agreed upon by such a diversity of interests."[37]

Yet his work as "Pluribus" in the Federalist Papers rarely spoke to religion and never as an advocate of a state religion to be designated in the new constitution. This would all come later in his life and during his fights with Jefferson and the states-rights advocates. It was during the elections of 1800 when Hamilton used the religion card to its greatest advantage.

Ever the political opportunist with his deep distrust of the non-federalists, specifically with Jefferson, Hamilton sided with the clergy against his foe. He spent a good amount of time prior to and during the 1800 presidential campaign asking if there were some steps permitted by law and the Constitution that would "prevent an atheist in religion from getting possession of the helm of state."[38] Hamilton was afraid that Jefferson, a deist and by some partisan newspaper accounts an atheist, may become president and remove religion completely from the new nation. This division accelerated as America entered into its first election without Washington and the unwitting creation of the two-party political system. Hamilton's arguments were not dissimilar from arguments today about the trustworthiness of an atheist or non-Christian politician.

Though Hamilton did champion Article VI of the Constitution in the Federalist Papers, his struggle against Jefferson in the faithful 1800 election was so strong that Hamilton wrote in the *Gazette of the United States* (a Federalist newspaper),

> At the present solemn moment the only question to be asked by every American, laying his hand on his heart, is "shall I continue in allegiance to GOD – AND A RELIGIOUS PRESIDENT; or impiously declare for JEFFERSON – AND NO GOD."

This is an argument still in use today as we follow the path of the

2012 presidential race. Many political candidates and pundits still take, as Hamilton did more than two-centuries earlier, great liberties in framing the election around religious belief.

In 1802, Hamilton, along with James Bradford, organized the Christian Constitutional Society. The objectives of the Society were stated in a letter to Bradford, in which Hamilton wrote,

> Let an association be formed to be denominated 'The Christian Constitutional Society,' its object to be:
>
> 1st. The support of the Christian religion.
>
> 2d. The support of the Constitution of the United States.
>
> My friends, we have waited awhile… in fact, we have waited too long, the time has now arrived, this is the offer to recover the Constitution our forefathers gave us as an inheritance, do with it what you will, but as for me I will make a stand for its preservation, it is our standard, it is our banner, it is our sword, to combat our political foes, just as the cross of Christ and the Word of God is our standard, banner, and sword to combat our spiritual foes.[39, 40]

There is little written about the original Society and it is most likely the idea died along with Hamilton, the day when he and Vice President Raymond Burr stood on the New Jersey shoreline in 1804 with their duelling pistols. There had been a recent attempt to re-establish the Christian Constitutional Society in the mid-2000s but it too seems to have fallen flat.

John Jay is one of the under-recognized and unsung Founders of our nation. Along with Hamilton and Madison, he was responsible for the

"Federalist Papers." He was also the first Chief Justice of the Supreme Court and set many precedent setting ruling during his tenure.

Jay's Anglican affiliation and participation was known to many. He was a lay officer at New York's Trinity Church, made famous after the 2001 terrorist attacks on the World Trade Center. He was a vice president and then president of the American Bible Society, arguing fervently for the abolition of slavery while, at the same time, arguing that Catholics should not be able to hold office in government.

His belief in the inerrant Bible and the Christian/ Anglican faith were solid and held since birth. Jay states as much in letters and discussions on religion. He notably distrusted Paine's *Age of Reason* as "it never appeared to me to have been written from a disinterested love of truth or of mankind."[41]

Friends of the John Jay Homestead write on their Web site, "The separation of Church and State was a radical concept in the late 18th century—that had never happened in the history of Western civilization. Jay felt strongly that the Church must not participate in the making of civil laws."[42] For Jay, devotion to God and his devotion to a secular government were equal kings.

The only mention of religion by Jay in the Federalist Papers is in No.2, "Concerning Dangers from Foreign Force and Influence for the Independent Journal." There he wrote:

> It has often given me pleasure to observe that independent America was not composed of detached and distant territories, but that one connected, fertile, wide spreading country was the portion of our western sons of liberty. Providence has in a particular manner blessed it with a variety of soils and productions, and watered it with innumerable streams, for the delight and accommodation of its inhabitants...

> With equal pleasure I have as often taken notice that Providence has been pleased to give this one connected country to one united people--a people descended from the same ancestors, speaking the same language, professing the same religion, attached to the same principles of government, very similar in their manners and customs, and who, by their joint counsels, arms, and efforts, fighting side by side throughout a long and bloody war, have nobly established general liberty and independence.

As for his thoughts on religion, Jay was incorrect in assuming that only one religion, Anglican, was represented in all colonies. Non-Christians had made their marks in all of the thirteen original colonies by 1780, and included Jews, Muslims, Catholics, deists and others.

Unfortunately Catholics were not deemed Christians and were targeted as "Popish followers," and not permitted to own property or participate in elections in many colonies and later states. This same distrust would raise its ugly head again during the rise of the anti-Catholic Ku Klux Klan in the early 1900s and openly later during the 1960 presidential elections.

The one quote that does indicate Jay's belief that the new country was founded as a Christian nation was made in 1797 in a letter to Jedidiah Morse, well after the writing of the Constitution and the Bill of Rights. "Providence has given to our people the choice of their rulers, and it is the duty, as well as the privilege and interest of our Christian nation to select and prefer Christians for their rulers."

This was a personal statement of position and interest, not one of national heritage or rule, and it definitely was not a declaration of the national psyche. There is no indication that Jay argued his religious agenda prior to his appointment to the Supreme Court. Even after his appointment, he maintained his principles and the course he had laid in life and the Constitution, by not using religion as a basis of his ruling.

༺༻

Conclusion

The Founders of this nation knew and, for the most part, agreed on one thing, that tyranny comes from absolute power and absolute power brings absolute tyranny. From their experience, absolute power comes when the church and the state are but one entity. Few, like Henry and Hamilton, argued differently and unsuccessfully.

This list continues for all of the original Founding patriots leading the battle for Independence, over 200 in all. Most understood, as Paine wrote, that a religion-based government would be and is a corrupt concept, and devoid of liberty. Many of the signers to the Constitution were pious, but almost all knew what the consequence would be if the federal government supported any single denomination. Through the document and its amendments, they chose to honor all religions, including those who professed no belief in God.

However, the religious affiliation of a large number of our Founders is unknown. Of the 56 signers of the Declaration of Independence, 15 either did not state a religious affiliation or their affiliation could not be verified.

So to say that the United States is a Christian nation based on the religious affiliations of the signers of the Declaration of Independents and the Constitution would simply be wrong.

Was the Constitution written as a result of religious, more specifically Christian, beliefs? Or was the new nation's government, our grand experiment in a representative-democracy, based on purely secular principles?

I believe I have shown here the latter is true. We are a pluralistic government that understood in 1776 and understands today that religion and government must live in harmonious independence and are yoked together only by necessity.

The Founders were very astute to leave God out of the only document that has any meaning to the construct of the United States of America, our Constitution. No religious tests to hold office, no state-established or supported religion, and no laws preventing the citizens from practicing the religion of non-religion of their choosing.

For further readings on religion and secular interaction and separation, I strongly suggest you visit either FindLaw.com or the Legal Information Institute of Cornell University Law School.

Chapter 7

Proclamations

ೞಌఴಌ

As with other proofs, there were a number of references to pre-Constitution quotes from documents supporting the Christian nation proponents' positions. Two proofs that appear to be prominent from the proponents are two resolutions to the Continental Congress, not the Congress of the United States, and are extremely important to this discussion. The first is a resolution presented by Samuel Adams. The second concerns our celebration of Thanksgiving as well as our national day of prayer. Both were usually quoted correctly, but do they have the power of "proof" that the United States was founded as a Christian nation?

ೞಌఴಌ

Oct. 12, 1778 - (A Resolution) Congress resolved; Whereas true religion and good morals are the only solid foundations of public liberty and happiness.

This quote comes as a part of the efforts to claim that patriot Samuel Adams, the cousin of President John Adams and a hero in his own right of the Revolutionary War, attempted to bring religion into the fold of government and the Continental Army. Ira Stroll's *Samuel Adams; A Life* provides the complete and correct citation of the resolution.

> Whereas true religion and good morals are the only solid foundations of public liberty and happiness;
>
> Resolved, That it be, and it is hereby earnestly recommended to the several states, to take the most effectual measures for the encouragement thereof, and for the suppressing theatrical entertainments, horse racing, gaming, and such other diversions as are productive of idleness, dissipation, and a general depravity of principles and manners.
>
> Resolved, That all officers in the army of the United States, be, and hereby strictly enjoined to see that the good and wholesome rules provided for the discountenancing of prophaneness and vice, and the preservation of morals among the soldiers, are duly and punctually observed.[1]

This was not Samuel Adams' attempt introduce God into the new nation's psyche, but to curtail what he saw as the officers of the state militias failing to maintain order of the troops. Many proponents miss the proposed effect of the resolution itself, to keep the troops from gambling, cavorting, and otherwise being preoccupied with something other than the war effort. The resolution put the officers on notice that they are responsible for their men's behavior.

Using religion as its base, Adams' declaration was not meant to include religion within the confines of government, but to use religion as a basis to corral the rude and ungentlemanly behavior among the troops. A careful reading finds that this is a recommendation only, not a law or proposed amendment to the Articles of Confederation; a distinction that seems to gets lost in the discussions.

In addition, Adams, though a pious man himself, did not mention which religion was the "true religion," apparently leaving that up to the officers and the troops (though it can be assumed it was a Christian sect).

This resolution occurred during the time prior to the Constitution. However, the Articles were the beginning, or at least the second attempt to establish an American government. The first was the Continental Congress. So for this discussion, it will be considered part of the founding of the national government we now enjoy.

Also lost is the fact that the Resolution did not receive a passing vote in the chambers of government.

As explained by David Collins, instructor of American History at Columbia College, the Articles of Confederation evolved directly from the Continental Congress. As the Revolution progressed, the leaders of the new nation decided that America needed a real government, so the Continental Congress quickly wrote new rules concerning the management of the new country, converting itself to the new Confederation of the United States. The purpose was two-fold. First, to receive formal recognition from other nations, most in conflict with Britain; second to acquire loans that could only be made to a sovereign nation.

Nowhere in the Articles is religion, Christianity, or God mentioned in terms of restrictions or freedoms, or as a source of inspiration. *Lord* is used in the context, as appropriate for the time, of designating the date. Though at the time most individual states sanctioned specific religions, and in each state the sanctioned religion was different, Article III of the Confederation stated that,

> The said States hereby severally enter into a firm league of friendship with each other, for their common defense, the security of their liberties, and their mutual and general welfare, binding themselves to assist each other, against all force offered to, or attacks made upon them, or any of them, on account of religion, sovereignty, trade, or any other pretense whatever.[2]

In other words, for the mutual protection and defense, including from religious persecutions resulting in armed action, internal or external. It can also be argued that the "security of their liberties" included the right to practice one's own religion; ensuring that right would not be limited or denied.

A second point concerning this resolution was the use of the term "morals." Was morality considered only through the eyes of the biblical commandments? The second paragraph of the proposed resolution makes it clear that these are not sectarian morals, but secular moral violations that produce, "idleness, dissipation, and a general depravity of principles and manners." Though a rough reference to scripture is made, there is no support that these vices could be controlled only through religious intervention alone but with the help the officers in charge.

A further reading indicates that this resolution was focused on the conduct of our fighting forces, not the public, and only is "earnestly recommended," not a demand or military rule. It would have made the officers responsible for maintaining discipline, preventing cursing, gambling, and womanizing. It is their conduct and the conduct of their troops which the resolution focuses.

Unlike his famous relatives who were Unitarians or Universalists, Samuel Adams was a Congressionalist and believed that temporal law is conceived through God. Yet his resolution does not mention God or

Christianity. It can be construed that God's hand was not at work in the drafting of this resolution and that the members of the assembly simply used the term "morals" in its secular state – that good and evil are based on knowledge, time, and experience, not on God.

Does the resolution of October 1778 validate the pro-Christian nation argument or does the reading of the full document discount such ideals?

At the time of the resolution, the feeding, arming, and clothing of the troops were the prime considerations. Discipline was near nonexistent. American soldiers frequently left the ranks to attend to family business, funerals, or parties. Any promise of being paid as a soldier in the war against England was more of a hope. So, unless the American troops became a more cohesive fighting force, the war would have surely been lost. This document was meant to make a bold statement concerning the poor morale among the troops

This resolution appears to be no more than an attempt to instill that discipline the American troops needed, to protect the Confederation, and to beat the pesky British. If this is so the case, then the answer to the question must be "no," this is not a "proof" of the Christian nation position. There appears to be no other position to take at this time, no contrary proofs supporting the proponents' stance.

༺༻

Oct. 18, 1780 - The first proclamation of a national day of thanksgiving and prayer, which concludes with these words, "...to cause the knowledge of Christianity to spread over all the earth."

The history concerning this proof is interesting and provides insight to the struggles that faced the new nation and of the American war for independence.

The 1780 day of thanksgiving and prayer was a proclamation made by the president of the Confederacy. However, according to the University of Virginia's "Papers of George Washington," not everyone was enamored with the idea of giving over a day for prayer concerning the war efforts.[3]

In its introduction, the editors of this UV paper state that Thomas Tudor Tucker believed "the House (of Burgess) had no business to interfere in a matter which did not concern them. Why should the President direct the people to do what, perhaps, they have no mind to do? If a day of thanksgiving must take place, let it be done by the authority of the several States."[4] Make the day a state holiday, not national.

Tucker's position was based on Locke's belief of the separation of religion and government, and he saw nothing in the Articles to support such a proclamation to be made by the President.

The proclamation of 1780 was a bit different from those made through the end of the war simply because of that final line. One must remember that this document was written in a style that was proper for any formal proclamation of the day, especially if the writers were under British authority.

> Whereas it hath pleased Almighty God, the Father of all mercies, amidst the vicissitudes and calamities of war, to bestow blessings on the people of these states, which call for their devout and thankful acknowledgments, more especially in the late remarkable interposition of his watchful providence, in rescuing the person of our Commander in Chief and the army from imminent dangers, at the moment when treason was ripened for execution; in prospering the labors of the husbandmen, and causing the earth to yield its increase in plentiful harvests; and, above all, in continuing to us the

enjoyment of the gospel of peace;

It is therefore recommended to the several states to set apart Thursday, the seventh day [of] December next, to be observed as a day of public thanksgiving and prayer; that all the people may assemble on that day to celebrate the praises of our Divine Benefactor; to confess our unworthiness of the least of his favors, and to offer our fervent supplications to the God of all grace;

...that it may please him to pardon our heinous transgressions and incline our hearts for the future to keep all his laws that it may please him still to afford us the blessing of health; to comfort and relieve our brethren who are any wise afflicted or distressed; to smile upon our husbandry and trade and establish the work of our hands; to direct our public councils, and lead our forces, by land and sea, to victory; to take our illustrious ally under his special protection, and favor our joint councils and exertions for the establishment of speedy and permanent peace; to cherish all schools and seminaries of education, build up his churches in their most holy faith and to cause the knowledge of Christianity to spread over all the earth.

Done in Congress, the lath day of October, 1780, and in the fifth year of the independence of the United States of America.

In essence, the proclamation was a form of propaganda,[5] using the faith of the predominantly Christian country to ask for divine intervention to save Washington and his troops, and to bring victory to the new nation. We see this same use of God as a tool of propaganda in many of America's great wars.

There were seven other proclamations for prayer and thanksgiving that did not demand spreading the faith. This was the only one of the eight proclamations prior to the signing of the Constitution in 1787 that did so. The authors of each declaration were astute in understanding that beliefs in a God were personal and could not and should not be forced by the state.

According to the Pilgrim Hall Museum, such proclamations were made annually between 1777 and 1784, but only one referred to the spread of Christian churches and faith.[6]

In examining all of the proclamations, "peace" is mentioned fifteen times, "independence" thirteen, and "liberty" six. God is mentioned eighteen times in the eight documents, so there is no doubt that there was an attempt by the authors in invoke God's blessing, but those blessings were for a victorious war effort and, in 1783 and 1784, for the success of the Treaty of Paris to bring the war of revolution to an end.

Each proclamation was, in fact, a prayer of the nation to an infinite God asking for his blessings in the American insurrection and for independence from the British. These are not declarations of law or of a national religion. There is no indication of establishing the new nation as Christian-based in law or substance.

By 1783 and 1784, the opening language of the proclamations had changed significantly, no longer focusing on "Almighty God" but a more deist view of religion. The prayer of thanks and blessings for a holding peace in 1783 begins,

> Whereas it hath pleased the Supreme Ruler of all human events, to dispose the hearts of the late belligerent powers to put a period to the effusion of human blood, by proclaiming a cessation of all hostilities by sea and land,

and these United States are not only happily rescued from the dangers distresses and calamities which they have so long and so magnanimously sustained to which they have been so long exposed, but their freedom, sovereignty and independence ultimately acknowledged by the king of Great Britain.

Once again, the proponents claiming this supports the Christian nation premise appear to be limited to a single line in a single proclamation, not as a statute or court rulings. In addition, the language used was proper for the time and, as a prayer, necessary to "ensure" acceptance by the body religion, the central point in many citizens' lives. The pulpit was used as much of a purveyor of the gospel as it was as the dispenser of news and of political vision. Read propaganda.

In 1784, without a clear direction as to the involvement of the state in church affairs or church in state's affairs, a proclamation of prayer would not have been unusual. Even today, the request of assistance from God in war and peace is heard on a regular basis from political officials. God's name is proclaimed by politicians in speeches and proclamations as relating the cause to the majority religion. Opening invocations are made by clergy in the chambers of Congress. Again, these are not done by statute but by habit and have little more than suggestive powers.

Does this proof provide the essence of a Christian nation? Again, it is difficult to make that connection. One statement made over an eight-year period does not hold as much weight as if it were stated every year, or by a legislative act or by the courts specifically weighing in on this issue. The argument made here does not seem to meet the criteria that these proofs are consistent and repeatable.

It must be noted that at no time do the proclamations mention any other specific Christian denomination as part of the prayers, though it can be assumed that the Anglican Church may have been the chosen sect. In his comments via email, author and historian Michael Adelberg mentioned that these proclamations may indicate a more moderate Christian support of "pluralism" than the notion of a Christian-based nation.

The controversy over a national day of prayer continues today. On April 29, 2011, President Barack Obama issued his proclamation for a day of prayer. But he had to by law.

In May of 1988, President Reagan signed into law Senate Bill 1378 that amended "Federal law to direct the President to set aside and proclaim the first Thursday in May in each year as a National Day of Prayer."[7] The title of the section marks a change in the ideal of church and state pluralism. Title 36 is called "Patriotic and National Observances, Ceremonies, and Organizations."

This is the only portion of 36 USC Chapter 1 that speaks to a day of religious observance and seems a bit awkward. Included in this list of almost three-dozen national observances are the Pan American Aviation Day, National Maritime Day, Patriot's Day, White Crane Safety Day, and the National Defense Transportation Day, to mention a few.

What is conspicuously missing from the list is Labor Day. That was done during the Cleveland administration as an appeasement to the labor unions after the infamous Pullman Strikes.[8] The Labor Day Act is found in 28 Stat. 96.

However, a new question is generated: Is a National Day of Prayer a violation of the First Amendment that the government appears to be sanctioning and supporting religion? This is a much tougher question than a simply "yes" or "no." Americans are not compelled to participate nor are there any obligations as to which religion or sectarian groups can and cannot participate. Yet, when discussing the matter of a national Day of Prayer many, Christian and non-Christian alike, believe that the prayers are to the Christian God and through the Christian faith even with no overt mention of Christianity.

This was evident when attending the May 4, 1978 prayer breakfast in Denver lead by President Jimmy Carter, an evangelical Christian, and Governor Richard Lamm, who still keeps his own religion private.[9]

Several hundred were in attendance in the Denver Convention Center and prayers were offered by several ministers, all asking for God's blessings on the State of Colorado and the United States. It was a "nondenominational" as a prayer meeting could become, but still maintain Christian overtones. Memory tells me that Judaism was not represented on the dais. However, I could be wrong.

Was this a violation of the First Amendment's separation doctrine? I will leave that one up to you.

Conclusion

The two examples provided here are by far not the only ones provided by the Christian nation proponents; however, they were the most prevalent of the proclamations quoted. Each cite showed that the quotes do exist and they are properly quoted, however, the quotes are taken out of context with the presenter, as with Samuel Adams, or the times, as with the need for a national prayer.

President Reagan's signature creating a National Day of Prayer was not one of the proponent's arguments, though I believe it would have been stronger and much harder to counter. The question remains whether 36 USC Chapter 1 acknowledgement of a National Day of Prayer is constitutional is still debated.

It is evident that the use of these prayers of thanks and national proclamations were not made to initiate or declare the United States as a Christian nation, but to address the citizenry in terms they most understood. It is also evident that the proclamations above planned to use the best method of communication of the time, the church pulpit. To accomplish the end, the means of communication was either print or voice and voice was just more applicable to the times.

Chapter 8

The Founding Papers

ଔଛଠ୰ଓଊ

An interesting discovery during this research was the number of documents referred to by the proponents and opponents of the Christian nation theories that are no long or have never been the "law of the land." In addition, few proponents referred to the Constitution in their arguments and none referred to the Articles of Confederation of the United States.

Though the Declaration of Independence is one of this nation's most important document, if read carefully it appears to be no more than a letter of complaint and resolution. The citizens and colonies had made their problems known to the Crown, however nothing was done. The colonies believed that they were reduced to non-citizens by King George and resulted in the colonies being left out of the governing conversations. Because these complaints had not been addressed except by the stationing of more British troops in America, an action needed to take place and that action was separating from Briton's rule and forming their own government.

However, the Declaration was not a document concerning how this new nation was to be organized. That came with the Articles of Confederation of the United States.

ಡಿಐಔಡಿ

The Articles of Confederation

The first "real" government of the new nation was the Confederation of The United States. "Real" because the Continental Congress had no formal document approved by the 13 original colonies from which to work.

The Articles of Confederation provided a foundation for the first government as it was signed and approved by representatives of the original thirteen colonies (Massachusetts and Maine were a single entity and Vermont was not yet established). This document was the key to a loosely knit national union of individual states. Again, according to historian David Collins, the Confederation was the immediate offshoot of the Continental Congress when, after the start of the war for independence, it was realized that the former colonies needed to have a unified central government to, among other things, get loans to pay for the war effort. America's first national debt.

On March 1, 1781, almost five years after the signing of the Declaration of Independence, the Articles of Confederation was signed and a national government established.[1] The Articles of Confederation is a short and concise document, maintaining that "Each state retains its sovereignty, freedom, and independence, and every power, jurisdiction, and right, which is not by this Confederation expressly delegated to the United States, in Congress assembled."[2]

By the mid 1770s each colony had an established church dominating the citizens of that state. The Founders well knew the problems with the theocratic-monarchies and -democracies of Europe and they wrote the Articles of Confederation to stipulate that no church would be nationalized. The states, however, were to permit their own recognized "official" churches.

Though each state was considered sovereign, each state also agreed to provide forces in mutual protection from attack. Article III of the Articles stated that each state was to, "assist each other, against all force offered to, or attacks made upon them, or any of them, *on account of religion*, sovereignty, trade, or any other pretense whatever." (Italics added)

Though there is little information available concerning the debate of this provision, if any, it is evident that the representatives from the various states saw freedom of religion on the same level as sovereignty and trade. This was a one of many precursors to the Bill of Rights and the First Amendment.

By 1784, Patrick Henry, a devout Anglican, turned away from ideal that the church and state were separate but equal partners. As a member of the Virginia Assembly, Henry would introduce the "Bill establishing a provision for Teachers of the Christian Religion."[3] Though today's conservative Christian community may believe that the purpose was to promote Christianity, thus proving the pro-Christian Nation position, the justification for the proposed law was to "restrain vice and preserve the peace." Though, or because, it used the language and the power of the Church to do so, it did not pass.[4]

CB♥♥CB

Memorial and Remonstrance

James Madison was one of the main forces who opposed Henry's proposed bill and it was Madison's June 20, 1785 "Memorial and Remonstrance" that may have been the definitive writing of the time concerning the issue of religion's involvement in government.[5]

Madison had collected over 1550 signatures supporting this documents and in opposition to Henry's proposal, setting yet another precursor for First Amendment to the Constitution and the liberties of beliefs.

Madison's opposition was simple; Patrick Henry's bill, and other similar bills, would encourage religious abuse without the oversight of the state. He also believed in the free will of man to believe as he felt fit.

> The Religion then of every man must be left to the conviction and conscience of every man; and it is the right of every man to exercise it as these may dictate. This right is in its nature an unalienable right.
> It is unalienable, because the opinions of men, depending only on the evidence contemplated by their own minds cannot follow the dictates of other men: It is unalienable also, because what is here a right towards men is a duty towards the Creator. It is the duty of every man to render to the Creator such homage and such only as he believes to be acceptable to him.[6]

> ...the Bill violates that equality which ought to be the basis of every law, and which is more indispensible, in proportion as the validity or expediency of any law is more liable to be impeached. If "all men are by nature equally free and independent," all men are to be considered as entering into Society on equal conditions; as relinquishing no more, and therefore retaining no less, one than another, of their natural rights.[7]

Madison's opposition on to Henry's proposal was most likely based, in part, on the ideals of his friend Thomas Jefferson. Jefferson's document was the "Virginian Act Establishing Religious Freedom."[8]

Virginia Act Establishing Religious Freedom

Written at about the same time as Madison's "Memorial," the Act was based on Jefferson's belief that the government should not infringe on the beliefs of the individual. Jefferson's incomparable work, which he believed was more important than the Declaration of Independence, recognized that "Almighty God hath created the free mind." He also knew that rulers, either of the church or of the government, were merely mortal.

> Having "assumed dominion over the faith of others, setting up their own opinions and modes of thinking as the only true and infallible, and as such endeavoring to impose them on others, hath established and maintained false religions over the greatest part of the world."

Though still not law, Jefferson and Madison were of the same ilk, as were most of the other Founders of the new nation. With the major exceptions of Alexander Hamilton and Patrick Henry, keeping the federal government out of personal religion as well as keeping religion out politics was paramount in the process of debating the new federal constitution. Jefferson called one's personal belief a "natural right" and believed that the lack of passage of the Virginia Act as an infringement of that right.

During the time of the American Enlightenment, deists became more involved in natural science and discovery than in the religious and what we may think of today as mythological beliefs of the religions of the time.

Though Patrick Henry's made his best efforts to incorporate religion into the national psyche later in his life, the legislators of

Virginia saw differently. Soundly argued, Jefferson's Act for Establishing Religious Freedom, with the aid of the persuasion power of James Madison, was approved by the Virginian House of Burgess in January of 1786. "The Act" was the final precursor to the First Amendment of the Constitution.

෬෫෨෮෬

The Federalist Papers

The 85 letters to the citizens of New York say little when it comes to religion's effects and connection to the new form of government. References to religion and God are found throughout the Federalist papers, but none of the statements show any proof that the Constitution was based on any religious zeal. In fact, in No. 18 written by Hamilton concerned the topic of religion of the ancient Greeks.

Though Christianity is mentioned in the 85 documents, it was not in an advocacy role. Christ was not mentioned, even with Hamilton as a state religion advocate, and James Madison's and John Jay's piousness, as the primary contributing reason for the new constitution. A search through Yale University's Avalon Project finds that the Federalist Papers remained mostly silent on the issue the religion of America under the new constitution, and virtually nothing concerning the Christianity of the nation is written.

This revelation must be put into perspective with the knowledge of the religious backgrounds of all three writers. All three were Anglicans who recognized that their beliefs where theirs and, with the exception of Hamilton later, saw the need of a secular government to derail any notion of turning America into an English or other European nation with their theocratic-monarchies or theocratic-democracies.

A reminder before we continue. The Federalist Papers were completed with the publishing on May 28, 1788 of No. 85 written by

Hamilton. It was not until 1789 and the First Congress when the amendments to the Constitution were proposed and sent to the various states for approval. As a result, the papers say nothing towards the first proposed amendment to the Constitution.

In Federalist Papers No. 1, Hamilton's introduction to the idea of a new nation was formulated. Here also is the first formal contemplation that political parties should not exist; an ideal Hamilton would forsaken by 1798.

Hamilton wrote, "For in politics, as in religion, it is equally absurd to aim at making proselytes by fire and sword. Heresies in either can rarely be cured by persecution."[9] Though he will change his mind about political parties and religion in politics, this is a very good indicator of the Founder's thinking at the time of presenting the federal Constitution to the citizens of a new nation.

Hamilton was also the author of No. 10. Again religion is only mentioned once. Most of the Christian nation proponents who quoted this letter tend to rely only on the first sentence of the paragraph. It is important, however, to read the entire designated paragraph to understand its true meaning. Note that many of the problems to which Hamilton refers in his letter to the citizen of New York are similar, if not the same, as we face today.

> *A zeal for different opinions concerning religion, concerning government, and many other points, as well of speculation as of practice; an attachment to different leaders ambitiously contending for pre-eminence and power*; or to persons of other descriptions whose fortunes have been interesting to the human passions, have, in turn, divided mankind into parties, inflamed them with mutual animosity, and rendered them much more disposed to vex and oppress

each other than to co-operate for their common good. So strong is this propensity of mankind to fall into mutual animosities, that where no substantial occasion presents itself, the most frivolous and fanciful distinctions have been sufficient to kindle their unfriendly passions and excite their most violent conflicts. But the most common and durable source of factions has been the various and unequal distribution of property. Those who hold and those who are without property have ever formed distinct interests in society. Those who are creditors, and those who are debtors, fall under a like discrimination. A landed interest, a manufacturing interest, a mercantile interest, a moneyed interest, with many lesser interests, grow up of necessity in civilized nations, and divide them into different classes, actuated by different sentiments and views. The regulation of these various and interfering interests forms the principal task of modern legislation, and involves the spirit of party and faction in the necessary and ordinary operations of the government. (Italics added)[10]

No. 18, co-written by Madison and Hamilton, was more a history lesson concerning the formation of a government by espousing the Greek democracies. Most notably, "Among the confederacies of antiquity, the most considerable was that of the Grecian republics, associated under the Amphictyonic council." Madison uses this lesson to support a stronger central government, as opposed to the state control of the Confederation of the United States.

The warning comes stronger when Madison speaks to the problem of a weak central government as found in the Articles of Confederation.

The powers, like those of the present Congress, were administered by deputies appointed wholly by the cities in their political capacities; and exercised over them in the same capacities. Hence the weakness, the disorders, and finally the destruction of the confederacy. The more powerful members, instead of being kept in awe and subordination, tyrannized successively over all the rest. Athens, as we learn from Demosthenes, was the arbiter of Greece seventy-three years. The Lacedaemonians next governed it twenty-nine years; at a subsequent period, after the battle of Leuctra, the Thebans had their turn of domination.[11, 12]

John Jay wrote Paper No. 2 telling the citizens of New York something sociologists understand very well today, that those who look alike, speak the same language and have the same belief system tend to stick together. In Jay's words;

With equal pleasure I have as often taken notice that Providence has been pleased to give this one connected country to one united people--a people descended from the same ancestors, speaking the same language, professing the same religion, attached to the same principles of government, very similar in their manners and customs, and who, by their joint counsels, arms, and efforts, fighting side by side throughout a long and bloody war, have nobly established general liberty and independence.[13]

This statement does show that the majority of emigrants to the New World were Europeans, steeped in various Christian faiths. This is not a statement, as others have argued, that the new nation was one of Christian faith, for multiple faiths were already represented in the colonies. My belief is that Jay did not misspeak here, but was looking at the individual cities and recognizing that enclaves were developing where peoples of the same religion and ethnicity gathered.

This same ethnic isolation can be seen today in all major cities, with their own designated enclaves. Be it "The Hill" in St. Louis or Little Italy, China Town, or the Hasidic section of Brooklyn in New York; even on larger college campuses throughout the country, those who look alike, sound alike and think alike tend to gather together for comfort and support.

Statements concerning religion found in Federalist Paper No. 5 concern a letter written by England's Queen Ann in 1706, speaking to the liberties of the new union between the people of Scotland and England. There is no further reference to the religion of the United States.

Hamilton's No. 31 speaks to the understanding of the new form of government in terms of science and of philosophy. Hamilton wrote,

> The objects of geometrical inquiry are so entirely abstracted from those pursuits which stir up and put in motion the unruly passions of the human heart, that mankind, without difficulty, adopt not only the more simple theorems of the science, but even those abstruse paradoxes which, however they may appear susceptible of demonstration, are at variance with the natural conceptions which the mind, without the aid of philosophy, would be led to entertain upon the subject. The INFINITE DIVISIBILITY of matter, or, in other words, the INFINITE divisibility of a FINITE thing, extending even to the minutest atom, is a point agreed among geometricians, though not less incomprehensible to common-sense than any of those

mysteries in religion, against which the batteries of infidelity have been so industriously leveled.[14] (Original emphasis maintained)

This is where the Christian theorists tend to stop in their argument. However, the next paragraph puts this seemingly confusing statement some perspective.

> Though it cannot be pretended that the principles of moral and political knowledge have, in general, the same degree of certainty with those of the mathematics, yet they have much better claims in this respect than, to judge from the conduct of men in particular situations, we should be disposed to allow them. The obscurity is much oftener in the passions and prejudices of the reasoner than in the subject. Men, upon too many occasions, do not give their own understandings fair play; but, yielding to some untoward bias, they entangle themselves in words and confound themselves in subtleties.

As you see, this section has nothing to do with religion, only the character of mortal men (and women) who have positions of power.

The final paper mentioning religion is No. 69 and is usually misquoted by the proponents of the Christian nation theories, conveniently removing six significant words.

Hamilton's 1788 document talks to the differences between the President of the United States and the monarchy of Great Britain, a fact conveniently left out by two of the respondents to my original requests for information. In this comparison, the President "has no particle of SPIRITUAL JURISDICTION," while the monarchy, "IS THE SUPREME HEAD AND GOVERNOR OF THE NATIONAL CHURCH!"[15] (Original emphasis maintained.)

Hamilton's conclusion; the new constitutional government whose "whole power of which would be in the hands of the elective and periodical servants of the people, is (not) an aristocracy, a monarchy, and a despotism."

Many historians and readers of the Papers are amazed at the solidarity of Hamilton, Jay and Madison on the topic of religion and the new constitution. Though there are discussions concerning religion, they are used as examples as to what will later be termed the separation of church and state. Though all three men were very religious, they did not speak to a national religion supported by the citizens through the collection of taxes. Though all were aware of the importance of states' rights, they also agreed that a strong federal government was important for the new nation to survive.

Therefore, there appears to be no evidence that the Federalist Papers supported a federally recognized religion or church.

ଔଛଡ଼ଔଔ

The Constitution

It is true that the Founders were highly educated men, many reading Greek and Latin as well as French. Baruch de Spinoza's views on ethics were well known by most, as were the writings of Thomas Hobbs, Jean-Jacques Rousseau and John Locke.

Hobbs' *Leviathan* spoke to the rule of government, that the sovereign should only led by the will of the people and the people, in a form of representative government, select a representative to convey the words of many to a council. It is the council that makes the rules concerning civil and property laws. If there is a breach of that law, then an independent judicial system would make a ruling based on that law.

Hobbs' continued by defining the three types of "commonwealths" as monarchies, aristocracies, and democracies. Though he does lean towards a democratic monarchy as the best form of commonwealth, his definitions helped create the idea of the representative democracy as we now have.

Rousseau's 1763 "The Social Contract" took a major step in defining the sovereignty of the individual and the purpose of government; to protect citizens' right to ownership of real property and an equal public voice in determining law.[16]

The text that seemed to have the greatest impact on the philosophy of the new government was John Locke's *Two Treatises of Government*, originally written circa 1690.[17] It is within the first of his two essays that Locke takes on the argument that monarchs must declare themselves as descendents of Adam, and God gave Adam the power to rule over all living things.

It is in Chapter 10 of the First Treatise where Locke makes the argument that a monarchy cannot be an inheritance from Adam, for one man cannot be King of the world. Kings have limited rule of their kingdoms and no more.[18]

Beginning the second essay, Locke boldly states, "It having been shewn in the fore going Discourse, 1°. That *Adman* [Adam] had not either natural Right of Fatherhood, or by positive Donation from God, any such Authority over his Children, or Dominion over the World as pretended."[19] In his time, this would be considered heresy and blasphemy.

Locke continued to argue that even if Adam had such dominion over all, that such power would have been long lost over the generations, and no one person can have the power over all the rest. The conclusion can only be drawn that Man has dominion over himself and nothing more.

When, as mentioned in the opening of this book, a student

suggested that the Constitution mentions God in 54 instances, my "this does not make sense" alarm rang and we scanned the document for any mention of God, Christ, Jesus, religion or any other similar term of which we could think. Language of religious nature of the country happens twice in the body of the document itself.

The first, and the most important, is found in Article VI, clause 3;

> The Senators and Representatives before mentioned, and the Members of the several State Legislatures, and all executive and judicial Officers, both of the United States and of the several States, shall be bound by Oath or Affirmation, to support this Constitution; *but no religious Test shall ever be required as a Qualification to any Office or public Trust under the United States.* (Italics added)

The Constitution declares that this federal mandate possibly was to be enforced on a state level as well as the federal. It is also important to recognize that the terms used in the Constitution are "Oath or Affirmation," giving full indication that one does not need to believe in any god or to be beholden to any other than to God to hold office or that one's oath to God was different than an affirmation to one's fellow citizens and the Constitution.

The wording of such an oath or affirmation is not defined by the Constitution. The exception is for the President of the United States. Even then, God is not mentioned in that oath - most likely purposely being left out. Article II, Section 1, clause 8 provides the words of the presidential oath:

> Before he enter on the Execution of his Office, he shall take the following Oath or Affirmation, "I do solemnly swear (or affirm) that I will faithfully execute the Office of President of the United States, and will to the best of

my Ability, preserve, protect and defend the Constitution of the United States."

Once again, the authors of this document noted that an affirmation could preserve the requirement of an oath. Indeed, it appears that the Founders may have believed that a person other than a Christian could one day be president.

With the passage of the Fourteenth Amendment, the Constitutional demands on the federal government were extended to the individual states.

None of the opponents of the Christian nation theories pointed out that the presidential oath does not include God as part of the oath. They did point out that there is no proof that George Washington used the phrase, "So help me God" at either of his swearings.[20]

We do know that adding the four-word phrase would have contradicted Washington's philosophy of church and state separation. French Foreign Minister Comte de Moustier, who attended the inauguration, transcribed the ceremony "verbatim," as was tradition at the time. "So help me God" is not found in his transcripts.

Washington's April 30, 1789 inauguration did set many precedents and tradition for future presidents, including the use of a bible. St. John's Masonic Lodge supplied that first bible when Chief Justice John Jay, who administered the oath, forgot to bring his. But a bible appears to have been used based only on Jay's piousness, not as an acknowledgement of a national religion.

The opening to and today's use of Genesis 49:13 was strictly a matter of chance and not purposely selected.

It is also true that other historians of the inauguration of the President, writing for the U.S. Senate, disagree with this position, indicating that Washington did say "so help me God" in taking the oath of office.[21]

According to the Senate's version of history,

> The Constitution only prescribes the oath that a President must take; it does not set forth the style or manner of the Inauguration. The nation's first inauguration established many precedents: Washington added the words, "So help me God" at the end of his oath; he kissed the Bible; and he delivered an Inaugural address, all of which have been followed by future Presidents.[22]

We do know that Franklin D. Roosevelt used the phrase, as has every President has since. We do not know who the first President was to say those four words. It is strongly suggested that it might have been John Adams, which makes more sense considering his piety to the Unitarian Church. We know that Thomas Jefferson and James Madison (remembering that Madison was also a pious man) did not.

We do know that "so help me God" is a personal statement, not one that binds the entire nation to a belief in any god or religious sect. It is the President who is swearing to God or asking for God's blessings, not any attempt to force the blessing on all Americans, as some profess.

The second statement of religion in is in Article VII, the signature line of the Constitution that declares that it was completed, "Convention by the Unanimous Consent of the States present the Seventeenth Day of September in the Year of our Lord one thousand seven hundred and Eighty..." Again, this is not a declaration of divine loyalty but merely the *pro forma* method of writing dates at that time.

The First Ten Amendments to the United States Constitution - "The Bill of Rights"

It was Patrick Henry and the anti-federalists who demanded that the new constitution guarantee specific rights that the new nation fought so hard to win. Henry's own proposed list of rights was amazing long, including assurances that citizens be permitted to practice their religion as they wished and be free from any mandated religion as desired by the new federal government. Once again this mandate did not extend to individual states to abide by this Amendment to the national governing document as the states were acknowledged as sovereign government bodies.

There were attempts to amend the body of the Constitution concerning religious freedom, however all failed. There were several versions of the provision preventing an establishment of a national religion, those included, "No religious sect or society in preference to others;" "Congress shall not make any law infringing the rights of conscience or establishing any religious sect or society..."[23]

The Constitution's amendments now include the "Establishment Clause" and "Free Exercise Clause." In a speech given in 1983 at Liberty Baptist College (now Liberty University), the late Senator Edward Kennedy reminded the students, faculty and administration of this conservative Christian university that "when the Constitution was ratified and then amended, the framers gave freedom for all religion, and from any established religion, the very first place in the Bill of Rights."[24]

Kennedy continued that the constitutional convention debates were kept secret and little has survived on what was debated and who said what. The historical meaning and extent of the debates can be found on Cornell University Law School's web site quoting from J. Story's "Commentaries on the Constitution of the United States."

"Probably," Story also wrote, "at the time of the adoption of the constitution and of the amendment to it, now under consideration, the general, if not the universal, sentiment in America was, that Christianity ought to receive encouragement from the state, so far as was not incompatible with the private rights of conscience, and the freedom of religious worship. An attempt to level all religions, and to make it a matter of state policy to hold all in utter indifference, would have created universal disapprobation, if not universal indignation."

The object of the religion clauses in this view was not to prevent governmental encouragement of religion, more specifically of Christianity, but to prevent religious persecution and to prevent a national establishment of any specific religion of denomination.[25]

೧෮෨෮෨

Jefferson's Wall

Christian nation proponents are correct in their statements that the Jefferson metaphor of the "wall of separation of church and state" simply do not exist within our Constitution. Both are found in letters written by Jefferson during and after his presidency.

The First Amendment does say five things. First, we have the right, within the limits of the law, to practice our personal religious beliefs as we please, including not believing in any god or mythology at all.

Second, the government is prevented from establishing or supporting any religion, or providing any preference towards any religious sect or denomination. This includes the more than 200 Christian denominations in the Unites States as well as Jewish, Muslim, Buddhist and other religious bodies you may discover in our pluralistic and diverse country. As our Founders argued, all religions, majority or minority, have equal standing in the eyes of the Constitution.

There is nothing in the First Amendment that prevents a person from praying in public places. Interpretations of the Amendment by the courts have declared that only the actual or appearance of sanctioning religion by the government is prohibited.

However, there seems to be a blind spot in these two statements and they are sometimes combined to read, "The courts are saying that a person cannot pray when and where they wish, especially in public buildings." There appears to be no basis for this position.

In contrast to some of the arguments put forth in this discussion concerning religion and the Constitution, agnostics, Wiccans and other non-Christian minority religions and associations were and are indeed protected by the same Constitution and Amendments as those professing Christianity, Judaism, or Islam.

The possible exception to these protections is atheism, which is not considered a religion in the eyes of U.S. law or by atheists themselves. Atheists rely on and are protected under the third section of the Amendment, freedom of speech. Additionally, The Civil Rights Act of 1964 reinforced this concept making atheists a protected class.[26]

Jefferson himself understood this issue too well, writing, "The legitimate powers of government extend to such acts only as are injurious to others. But it does me no injury for my neighbor to say there are twenty gods or no God. It neither picks my pocket nor breaks my leg." Being an atheist, agnostic, deist, or even a Pastafarian was okay in Jefferson's eyes.[27]

Third is our right to pronounce our opinions without retaliation by the government, again with some expressed exceptions.[28] This "right" extends to secular and sectarian pronouncements, mainstream press and the citizen journalists -bloggers- and arguments for and against God and science. It is our right to speak our mind, whether or not anyone else agrees. This is as true for the Westboro Baptist Church, whose fellowship protests homosexuality at military funerals, as it is atheists proclaiming that God and the various holy writings are myths.

Here is where the arguments, especially since 2001, have become ugly and extremely partisan. Some conservative-Christians, the "squeakier wheels," claim that atheists and "liberals" wish to remove religion from the government and prevent religion from being practiced. This is simply wrong. Like other groups, there are those who sit on the extreme of the church-state separation issue, but the elimination of religion or beliefs in myths would be near impossible and a point that most church-state separation advocates understand.

അഃഃരു

Treaty of Peace and Friendship between the United States of America and the Bey and Subjects of Tripoli, of Barbary

This document is the most frequently quoted by the opponents of the Christian nation theories as proof that the United States was not founded as a Christian nation.

For decades the northern African states on the Barbary Coast were forcibly boarding merchant ships in the Mediterranean, some of which originated in and flew the flag of the United States. By 1785, the Confederation had allocated $80,000 "to continue treaties" with Algiers, Morocco, Tripoli and Tunis. In reality, the monies were meant to pay the ransom or tribute for the return of the American vessel *Betsy* and her crew seized in 1784. By July of that same year, Algiers seized two more American merchant ships and declared war on the United States. By 1786, at least 21 Americans were being held as slaves in Algiers with all attempts to seek their release unsuccessful.

Fast forward to 1793 when Algiers seized eleven more American vessels, including the American brigantine *Polly*, taking 119 American sailors prisoner. Algiers demanded a ransom of $1,000,000 (almost $42 million in 2011 dollars) for the return of the *Polly*. Allegedly, the ransom was paid by a Jewish merchant living in Algiers on behalf of the new American government.

With the state of war already existing (and considering the time it took for news to travel from Europe to America), President Washington authorized the building of six frigates to defend American shipping, thus giving birth to the United States Marines. (The battles in and around Tripoli have been forever memorialized in the Marine Hymn, "From the Halls of Montezuma to the shores of Tripoli...")

By 1795, the Barbary States had had enough of the American offensive and negotiations began on what is known today as the Treaty with Tripoli, ratified by the Senate and signed by President John Adams.

Article VI, Clause 2 of the Constitution is unequivocal in its purpose.

> "This Constitution, and the Laws of the United States which shall be made in Pursuance thereof; *and all Treaties made, or which shall be made, under the Authority of the United States, shall be the supreme Law of the Land*; and the Judges in every State shall be bound thereby, any Thing in the Constitution or Laws of any State to the Contrary notwithstanding." (Italics added)

Article 11 of the Treaty with Tripoli is also unambiguous in its language.

> *As the government of the United States of America is*

not in any sense founded on the Christian Religion, as it has in itself no character of enmity against the laws, religion or tranquility of Musselmen, and as the said States never have entered into any war or act of hostility against any Mehomitan nation, it is declared by the parties that no pretext arising from religious opinions shall ever produce an interruption of the harmony existing between the two countries. (Italics added)

The nature of the treaty's statement concerning religion and that the Constitution made the treaty the "supreme law of the land," provides the strongest statement by the Founders of the United States, many representing their states as members of the new federal government. The language remaines strong and unequivocal - The United States was not founded as a Christian nation.

There is one possible argument against the language in the treaty that the Christian nation proponents fail to address - that the Treaty of Tripoli was only in effect for ten-years. The proponents could have argued, but did not, that Article 11 of the treaty no longer has legal standing.

Discussions with a number of Constitution law scholars and historians seem to negate this argument based on a single reason. The United States did not cancel the treaty. Its cancellation was caused when the pirates of the Barbary once again attacked American and European shipping without provocation. Based on this fact, the contents of the original treaty cannot be ignored as simply "invalid." That portion of the treaty was and still is a definition of the American premise concerning religious freedom and tolerance made in a time when many of the originators of the Constitution were still alive.

Conclusion

There appears to be no evidence that these documents, cited by proponents and opponents alike, holds that our nation founded on Christian values. On the contrary, due to the lack of any mention of the Christian, Jewish and Islamic God, the only conclusion that can be drawn is that none of these documents were motivated by a church or religious order and that the government of the United States was secular in nation.

Chapter 9

God and the Constitution

ଔଽଠଃଠଔ

The Six, Ten, Twelve, Fifteen or 613 Commandments

During a college classroom discussion on the Constitution, a bold statement was made by one student, that American law, more specifically the Constitution, is based on the Ten Commandments. Not all in the class agreed, but it was a subject worthy of examination.

The question that I will use to start that discussion is the same I will use here; "Which version of the Ten Commandments?" And then there is always, "Weren't there originally 15?" This is not based on Mel Brook's "History of the World, Part I," but upon the stories given in Exodus and Deuteronomy.[1]

Why is this seemingly awkward discussion relevant to the topic at hand? Two reasons. First the proofs, most unsupported, that the Constitution and the Declaration were based on the Ten Commandments are cited by many of the proponents.

Second, not every Western religion or sect believes in the same Ten Commandments. The accepted Jewish Commandments are a bit different from the Catholics, which are a bit different from the Protestants, and so on down the line. If, as argued by some ardent proponents of the Christian nation theories, that the Constitution was based on religious, and more specifically Christian beliefs as noted in the Ten Commandments, one must ask, "Which ten?"

On August 26, 2003, on SFGate.com Don Lattin, the San Francisco Chronicle's religion reporter, jokingly started its column, "Just which commandments are the 10 Commandments?"[2] Lattin's question led him to several observations concerning sectarian law.

> You've got your Jewish Ten Commandments, your Catholic Ten Commandments, your Lutheran Ten Commandments, your Charlton Heston Ten Command-ments, your King James Bible Ten Commandments, your New Revised Standard Version Ten Commandments, and they don't all agree as to which commandment is which -- or what they really mean.[3]

Even the Torah contains three versions of the Commandments, one in Exodus 20, another in Exodus 34, and still a third version in Deuteronomy 5:6-21. This does not include, of course, the various English translations from ancient Hebrew, Arabic, Latin and Greek texts.

Further complicating the Commandments issue is the fact that neither of the Exodus versions neatly numbered the Commandments from one to ten. Translators numbered them in an order as they appear in the texts. Deuteronomy's version seems to have twelve commandments, not ten, and differs from the two found in Exodus. By combining and shuffling the three, you may get more than fifteen.[4]

The fifteen Commandments also come from the various religious translations and the three biblical origins of the originals, each with some manipulation to meet specific needs of each sect. For example, Sam Shamoun wrote on www.answering-islam.org suggesting that the fifteen may be due to a misreading of the Qur'an and the translation into English. However, if one reads Exodus 20 and 34 and Deuteronomy 5, you can find fifteen commandments in all - maybe more.

If "Commandments" is taken to mean the laws that must be followed because they are the Word of God, reading the Talmud, the traditional Jewish book of laws, you will find 613 "laws" that must be followed.[5] So, are we speaking of 10, 12, 15 or 613 Commandments? More? Less?

In Jesus' Sermon on the Mount, only six Commandments are mentioned.

In Matthew 5:18, Jesus tells his followers, "For truly I tell you, until heaven and earth disappear, not the smallest letter, not the least stroke of a pen, will by any means disappear from the Law until everything is accomplished."

In Matthew 5:21-48, and 6:1-4, Jesus sets forth the six commandments:

1. *Do not murder or curse your brother or sister.* I presume this to mean all men and women.
2. *Do not commit adultery.* But this commandment also puts full blame of the crime of adultery on the woman and though the quote does not prohibit divorce, it does label any divorced woman as an adulterer.
3. *Do not break your oaths or promises.* In fact, Jesus tells us never to make any promise or oath for fear of evil.
4. *Do treat your enemy fairly.* This does not say that one should punish an "eye for an eye and a tooth for a tooth," but to turn the other cheek, treat all fairly, and prove yourself a better

person than the person treating you ill. (Matthew 5:38-39)

5. *Do pray for and love your enemy.* Here the Gospel is clear; even the pagans complied with this thought, it is not strictly God's Words for his newest followers.

6. *Do give to the needy.* But do it without bragging or seeking attention.

Then the list continues through Chapters 6 of the Sermon. What to say when you pray, how does one fast, not to horde treasures, and, most important in this chapter, don't worry, be happy. And the list continues through Matthew 7. If one would count all of these as "commandments," our list has grown to 15 or 16.

Which version of the Commandments? The Catholic, Protestant, and Hebrew versions are all a bit different in order, wording, and interpretation.[6] Which version of the Christian Bible: NIV, KJV, New World, New American... the list goes on. The translations can differ greatly. As mentioned above, which set of tablets, the first given to Moses or the second?

In fact, the Exodus 34 version calls for the keeping of Passover and eating Kosher, or that which is good, is not found in Exodus 20.

The Eucharist, the bread representing the body and the wine the blood of Christ, appear to be in conflict with the Seventh Commandment of the Exodus 34 version, "Thou shalt not offer the blood of my sacrifice with leavened bread." This is pre-Christian, but Jesus did call for all to follow the laws of God as they were written in the Torah of the time.

Using the King James Version of the Ten Commandments and examining the U.S. Constitution, there appears to be no correlation. None of the Commandments that speak to man's relationship to God are mentioned in the Constitution. They are not even implied.

The secular laws found in each version of the Commandments, do not steal, do not commit adultery, do not bear false witness, and do not "covet" your neighbor's property, are not mentioned in the Constitution. The Constitution does speak to a person's right not to bear witness against oneself (Amendment V).

America's basic local, state and federal laws that appear to connect with the last four Commandments happen to be universal, the same basic laws found worldwide, even in those "godless commie" countries of the former Soviet Union, today's Russia, China and Cuba.

There were similar laws before the time of Moses, found in Babylon, Egypt, Samaria and many other pre-Hebrew societies. To many, these are "Humanist" laws, basic to the needs of any moral society.

Alan Dershowitz in his book *Rights from Wrongs: A Secular Theory of the Origins of Rights* suggests that morality is not based on biblical law, but on temporal experiences, increase in knowledge, and changes within a society.[7]

Dershowitz, who also wrote *Blasphemy: How the Religious Right is Hijacking the Declaration of Independence*, is a controversial figure when it comes to the more liberal side of morality, religion, and church and state issues. This is not to say he is anti-Christian, but his politics and philosophy appear to lean heavily towards a secular based society. Many agree with Dershowitz and there are many who do not, with some liberals and some conservatives denouncing Dershowitz as a "kook."[8] Others, a genius.

૭૪૭૪૭૪

The Great Disconnect

For many Christian nation proponents, there appears to be a great disconnect between the idea of a Christian based government in the

United State, a theocratic-democracy and a theocratic government. For others, any threat to their Christian faith or their understanding or conception that the United States as a Christian nation is taken as a crossing of the Rubicon, as an attack on Christianity and our nation.

German clergyman Pastor Martin Niehmoller (1892 – 1984) recognized this disconnect during the Second World War. In the beginning of the war he initially supported the National Socialist German Workers' (Nazi) Party.[9] In 1936, the German government made the church subordinate to state authority and, in protest the following year, Niehmoller began the "Pastors' Emergency League." He was arrested twice and spent his last seven years of the war in the concentration camp of Dachau. In the years after the war, Niehmoller went back to the church, eventually being elected as the President of the World Council of Churches.

As the well documented story goes, during a lecture a student asked Niehmoller a simple and unambiguous question, "How did it happen?" His response was direct and clear.

> "First they came for the Communists, but I was not a Communist so I did not speak out. Then they came for the Socialists and the Trade Unionists, but I was neither, so I did not speak out. Then they came for the Jews, but I was not a Jew so I did not speak out. And when they came for me, there was no one left to speak out for me."[10]

Questions must be asked; "Which Christian sect will be the dominant church, the one that would eventually control the powers of the government?

༄༅༅༅

Constitutional Language

Are we to forget the two most important sections of the

Constitution as it concerns this discussion?

The first is Article VI, clause 3 stipulating that "no religious Test shall ever be required as a Qualification to any Office or public Trust under the United States." The second is, of course, the First Amendment, "Congress shall make no law respecting an establishment of religion, or prohibiting the free exercise thereof...," a demanding Right that not only frees us from an established state religion but also provides us with the ability to practice our own beliefs, even if that belief is atheistic. It asks that all Americans be tolerant of all religions, Christian, Jewish, Islamic, Hindu, Buddhist or otherwise - even atheists, agnostics and Wiccans - and not to cause laws that would infringe these rights.

On September 17, 2010, former Speaker of the House and 2012 presidential candidate Newt Gingrich addressed the fifth annual Valued Voter Summit in Washington, D.C. This politically, religiously, and socially conservative group met with about 40 speakers, many whom were would-be presidential hopefuls. Breakout sessions included "American Apocalypse--When Christians Do Nothing, Secularists Do Everything--The Case for Christian Activism," "A Special Polling Presentation: Who are Tea Party and Christian Voters and What Do They Believe?," "Establishing a Culture Impact Team In Your Church," and "Why Christians Should Support Israel."[11]

CNN reported that Gingrich attacked the current administration, stating, "'On the one front we have a secular socialist machine led by (President) Obama, (House Speaker Nancy) Pelosi, and (Senate Majority Leader Harry) Reid, and on the other front we have radical Islamists who would fundamentally change this country into a system none of us in this room would recognize.' He received thunderous applause."[12]

Gingrich's overt remarks mixing religion and government leans towards a dangerous precedent. Dr. Gingrich should understand the problems theocracies had in Europe and the Americas over the ages and what has happened in the Middle-East and Asian subcontinent. Was the idea that the American political society has only a choice between a godless secular, or Islamic government, or a theocratic Christian democracy? And what would that something else look like? A Christian based political system? Many who oppose the Christian nation sentiment believe that it was exactly that which Gingrich was speaking.

In his 1983 address to Jerry Farwell's Liberty Baptist Church, Senator Edward "Ted" Kennedy spoke to the tolerance and plurality of the American government. He said in his speech entitled "Truth and Tolerance in America."

> A generation ago, a presidential candidate had to prove his independence of undue religious influence in public life, and he had to do so partly at the insistence of evangelical Protestants. John Kennedy said at that time: "I believe in an America where there is no religious bloc voting of any kind." Only twenty years later, another candidate was appealing to a[n] evangelical meeting as a religious bloc. Ronald Reagan said to 15,000 evangelicals at the Roundtable in Dallas: "I know that you can't endorse me. I want you to know I endorse you and what you are doing."
>
> To many Americans, that pledge was a sign and a symbol of a dangerous breakdown in the separation of church and state. Yet this principle, as vital as it is, is not a simplistic and rigid command. Separation of church and state cannot mean an absolute separation between moral principles and political power. The

challenge today is to recall the origin of the principle, to define its purpose, and refine its application to the politics of the present.[13]

After speaking of the religious discrimination legislated by the various colonies of the new nation, Kennedy said, "But during the Revolution, Catholics, Jews, and Non-Conformists all rallied to the cause and fought valiantly for the American commonwealth -- for John Winthrop's 'City Upon a Hill.' Afterwards, when the Constitution was ratified and then amended, the framers gave freedom for all religion, and from any established religion, the very first place in the Bill of Rights."

The statement was not to elevate the worthiness of President John F. Kennedy. It was to show the danger of eliminating the secular principles of a pluralistic government as set by the Founders of this great nation and why religious tolerance is so important in this nation. It was to show why our government must recognize the secular powers without denying one's rights to believe in their chosen faith or in no faith at all.

Kennedy continued, "The real transgression occurs when religion wants government to tell citizens how to live uniquely personal parts of their lives."

Today, questions concerning abortion, nuclear armament treaties, the death penalty, and other moral issues are argued on religious principles by many conservative-Christians, not considering the principle of the individual or national consciousness. This appears to be contrary to the Founders beliefs that as long as our disagreements remain secular in nature, the United States remains different than many other nations of this planet.

Some Christian nation proponents subscribe to misinformation and the use of propaganda; they appear to be to convince that the secular half of our pluralistic government is somehow wrong and dangerous. Yet, once again, Jesus himself recognized the need for temporal law in Matthew 22.

But things seem to be changing. During the turmoil in Northern Africa and Middle Eastern states in 2011, known as the Arab Spring, those who were protesting the totalitarian regimes are now establishing secular and democratic governments. Not like the United States, but like Turkey, Mustafa "Ataturk" Kemal's secular republic which has been truly pluralistic since 1924.[14]

Even after the 1980 military coup and the 1982 Constitution, Turkey remains a democratic, secular and parliamentary government system. With over 95 percent of its citizens of the various Muslim sects, Turkey's success is seen as a political and foundation of future Islamic sectarian harmony by most reform movements in the region.

༺༻

The Foreseeable Dangers

Professing that the United States was founded on Judeo-Christian principles is by itself not dangerous. The fact that there is simply no evidence to support that position is noteworthy.

However, when people act to drown out other faiths, including deists, agnostics, atheists, Muslims, and other Christian denominations that do not fit their "mold" and do not agree with the majority faith, we are in danger of forfeiting the principles on which this country is based; free religion and free speech.

As we have seen, the arguments made by those whom are identified as the proponents of the Christian nation theories, the seemingly religious nationalists, are mostly incorrect. These include many of the Christian-conservative politicians seeking the Republican presidential candidacy in 2012, including Newt Gingrich, Michelle Bachman, Gov.

Rick Perry and others.

It is obvious that too few have taken the time to look up the arguments they profess and verify the information. It is not that the words are not there, it is that they are not the words that set precedent. It is not that their knowledge of American history is wrong, but it may be incomplete or misdirected.

In the introduction, I mentioned a young lady whose minister told her that God was mentioned in the Constitution 54 times. When we discovered together that her minister was mistaken, she asked why her minister lied. I do not think he did, but do believe that he was misinformed and did not verify the information. I think this is the same situation in which many proponents of the Christian Nation side find themselves. This was one of the best self-edifying lessons in critical thinking I have witnessed.

Many of our Founders were Christians, but they lived in a time when Church and State were one and the same in most European nations. The Founders recognized the problems caused by such a marriage, as they saw the problem with a monarchy style government. They also knew when religion and government were combined, dangers lurked in the shadows. With few exceptions, they wanted to avoid that mistake.

That sentiment was so universal by 1787 that Alexander Hamilton, John Jay, and John Adams did not discuss religion or God in the *Federalist Papers*. There are no records of in-depth discussions concerning church/state status in the various constitutional conventions. It was not necessary because the nation knew that sectarian and secular law must remain in their appropriate houses.

The experiments in Rhode Island and Virginia concerning religious freedom and tolerance, along with the separation of sectarian and secular law were successful. Though Jefferson was in France at the time of the writing of the Constitution and the Bill of Rights, his Virginia Act for Establishing Religious Freedoms became the basis of the first sentence of the First Amendment.

༄༅༅༄

Conclusion

In November, 2010, Eddie Filer, writing for the NapleNews.com Web site said,

> In order to be classified as a Christian nation, it seems to me that the country would have to set up Jesus Christ as their ruler and do what he commanded. There could be no voting for men who have different ideologies as to how the country is to be governed.
>
> Some people equate Christianity with pledging allegiance to the flag and with other forms of outward patriotism. Jesus said nothing about any country being a Christian nation.[15]

I strongly agree with this statement. There appears to be no evidence otherwise.

We cannot hold to the self-evident truth "that all men are created equal" if we treat our neighbors differently because they enjoy a different interpretation of the scriptures, have different scriptures or no scriptures at all. We cannot force the citizens of this nation or any nation to accept a religious or theocratic belief without destroying the foundation of the United States.

There appears to be no connection, either direct or indirect, to the Constitution of the United States and any version of the Ten Commandments provided by the Christian nation proponents. There is no constitutional requirement to honor our parents, to believe in one god, no less a specific god, or to keep the Sabbath.

This conclusion includes the first ten amendments of the Constitution, the Bill of Rights, and of any amendment considered thereafter.

Are the advocates for a Christian nation lying or misrepresenting the documents? I do not believe so. There is a deep want by the proponents to find the proofs regardless of or lack of the connection. This want becomes the "truth" and the information that they have been provided by men and women of power and knowledge want them to believe appears to be the sole source of justification. And belief is much stronger than fact when the personal belief is challenged.

Chapter 10

In God We Trust

ଓଧ୍ୟ

As we continue this discussion, it would be remiss if we did not tackle the issue of the most visible arguments for the Christian nation theory proponents that the United States is today a Christian nation: Our money and our national pledge, as well as Lincoln's *Gettysburg Address*.

Many look towards Francis Scott Key's poem of the siege of Fort McHenry and the first of four stanzas, our National Anthem, as proof of the nation's religiosity. Still others firmly believe that "God Bless America," written by a Jewish immigrant as a show tune and made famous on the radio, should be the U.S.'s new national anthem.

Part of the proponent's argument for Christian nation status is the fact that God shows up on our money and in our pledge, a fact not lost on world citizens. Canada and England also have God's blessings written upon their money, and in their anthems and pledges, but the United States seems to take a stronger stance on the idea than our two closest allies.

The Star Spangled Banner

This story begins with Francis Scott Key's poem.

The original poem that became our national anthem consists of four stanzas, not the one we have come to love. And the first stanza is not exactly the same as the anthem we sing before baseball games and NASCAR races. Key had question marks where we put exclamation points and this seems to change the meaning of each sentence, though not the overall sentiment of the anthem itself. Additionally, "The Star Spangled Banner" was not the name of the original poem either. It was the "Defense of Fort McHenry."

> Oh, say, can you see, by the dawn's early light,
> What so proudly we hail'd at the twilight's last gleaming?
> Whose broad stripes and bright stars, thro' the perilous fight,
> O'er the ramparts we watch'd, were so gallantly streaming?
> And the rocket's red glare, the bombs bursting in air,
> Gave proof thro' the night that our flag was still there.
> Oh, say, does that Star-Spangled Banner yet wave
> O'er the land of the free and the home of the brave?

It does not quite match the music with the question marks, does it?

The story is one familiar to most.[1] It was during the War of 1812; the British had again come ashore in battle against America. In September 1814, Key and friend John Skinner negotiated the successful release of American civilian prisoners from British custody. However, the British were fearful of Key and Skinner would tell the American army of the British plans to attack Fort McHenry and held the two on one of the British warships. The attack began on September 12 with land forces. At 6:30 A.M. on September 13, the British began their naval bombardment of McHenry.

For 25 hours, the British continued their assault. On the morning of the fourteenth, the commander of McHenry, Major George Armistead, raised the 30 by 40 foot garrison flag as a sign of defiance of the British, prompting Key's line "Oh, say, can you see, by the dawn's early light/ What so proudly we hail'd at the twilight's last gleaming?"

Though the last stanza of the poem states "In God is our trust," this was not meant as an assignment of religion to a nation, but the statement of one writer and patriot of the second war against the British.

That God is not mentioned in the first stanza, or the next two, which may be a possible reason why "God Bless America" has become so important to the conservative and Christian political movements, and the unofficial anthem for baseball, football, hockey, and NASCAR today.

God Bless America was written by a Jewish immigrant from Russia, Irving Berlin, who wrote the original version "1918 at Camp Upton, located in Yaphank, Long Island, for his Ziegfeld-style revue, Yip, Yip, Yaphank."[2] Realizing that a second major European conflict had begun, Berlin rewrote the music and lyrics and reintroduced the music in 1938, not as much as a song of God's blessings to win a war as it was a song for peace. It was Kate Smith who sang the song of peace on Armistice Day, 1938 and it became hers.

☙❧

National Motto

Regardless of why Key wrote "In God is our trust" in the last stanza of his poem, it is evident that this not a call for a Christian nation, but a calling to one man's god for reassurance that America, and specifically Fort McHenry, would survive. The poem was a conversation between Key and the American citizenry.

It would take another 140 years before "In God We Trust" would become official. The *de facto* first motto of the nation, *E Pluribus Unum*, which is also found on our currency, does not refer to God but to the people. Like other stories, this one starts much earlier in our short history.

After the signing of the Declaration of Independence, the Continental Congress set up a committee to design a national emblem for the new nation, a national seal. The primary focus of the national seal was on the undivided unity of the new nation. The committee members included Thomas Jefferson, Benjamin Franklin and John Adams, with Jefferson the main contributor to the "observed" (front) side and Franklin of the "reverse." Franklin's design was the now familiar pyramid with the "all seeing eye."[3] Of course, the pyramid and eye have spawned many a conspiracy theory itself concerning the Freemasons taking over the world. But that is a different book.

The *de facto* national motto found on the observed side was, and still is, "*E Pluribus Unum*," "Out of Many, One."[4] Embroidered over the American bald eagle, the phrase came from "The Gentleman's Magazine," a literary magazine which used the motto as part of its own masthead. Pierre Eugene du Simitiere first suggested the motto to the committee and Jefferson picked up on the idea and incorporated *E Pluribus Unum* into his original design for the observed side of the Great Seal.

Why *de facto*? Though ordered by the Continental Congress, the motto was never formally recognized by either the Confederation or the Federal congresses of the United States as its national motto. That did not happen until 1956 at the height of the Cold War with the passage of

House Joint Resolution 396 making "In God We Trust" the formal motto of the United States of America.

It was in 1782 when Charles Thomason added an annotation that some have declared as an acknowledgement of God on the Great Seal. "*Annuit cœptis,*" translates from the Latin to "Providence favors our undertakings," was added to the top standard of the reverse of the Seal.

"*Annuit*" can also be translated to "He" or "God," but those are looser translations of the Latin. Providence, thought by many to refer to God or a deity, may also mean "the proper and due diligent management," which is something that may be more in line with Jeffersonian pluralistic thinking.

Finally, "*Novus ordo seclorum,*" found on the bottom of the reverse side of the Seal, translates to "A new order for the ages," and is yet another part of the Freemason conspiracy theories, but more likely refers to the new form of government.

Many proponents of the Christian nation position take the looser translation of *annuit* as a "proof" and evidence of their position. As discussed earlier, deists like Jefferson and Franklin, and those of various Christianity sects such as Adams, Monroe and other Founders of faith, did not want religion to be a factor in the new government. Their collective belief in "Providence" was that of something larger than man's imagination could devise or of the diligent undertaking of government. The latter translation, along with "*E Pluribus Unum*" and "*Novus ordo seclorum,*" are the best indicators that religion, especially the Christian religions, was not part of the development of the new government. The Founders wanted a proper and diligent management of the new order that they saw in the American experiment.

CR☙❧CR

On the Money

In 1837 Congress passed an Act that restricted the Department of the Treasury from making any changes to United States coinage without the consent of Congress. It is that Act which turned the tide on the money.

In January 1861 the southern states began their secessions from the Union and by February, the Confederate Constitution was written, naming Jefferson Davis as the provisional president of the Confederacy. In April, President Lincoln informed South Carolina that he was sending supplies to Fort Sumner, thinking it would avert a conflict. On April 12, Southern forces attacked the fort and the Civil War began.[5] The rest is history.

(This may be in contradiction with Tony Howitz's 2011 *Midnight Rising: John Brown and the Raid That Sparked the Civil War,* and others who postulate that it was John Brown's attempted siege of Harper's Ferry in 1859 that started the conflict.)

The United States was in a cycle of increased piousness in the years leading up to the Civil War.[6] On November 13, 1861, Secretary of the Treasury Salmon P. Chase received a letter from the Rev. M. R. Watkinson, Minister of the Gospel from Ridleyville, Pennsylvania, one of many letters sent to the Treasury with suggestions for designs of the new coinage. Rev. Watkinson's letter made a bold suggestion. Reverend Watkinson wrote,

> You (Mr. Chase) are probably a Christian. What if our Republic were not shattered beyond reconstruction? Would not the antiquaries of succeeding centuries rightly reason from our past that we were a heathen nation? What I propose is that instead of the goddess of liberty we shall have next inside the 13 stars a ring

inscribed with the words PERPETUAL UNION; within the ring the all seeing eye, crowned with a halo; beneath this eye the American flag, bearing in its field stars equal to the number of the States united; in the folds of the bars the words GOD, LIBERTY, LAW.[7]

On November 20, Chase ordered the director of the Philadelphia Mint, James Pollock, to come up with some suggestions for the statement that would eventually appear in the "folds of the bars." Pollack forwarded two mottos that were reviewed by Chase, who made a few small revisions. The now familiar "In God We Trust" was approved by Chase and sent to Congress, which approved the new design with its new language in April, 1864. It first appeared on the Union's two-cent coinage later in the year, but was not a regular feature on our money for another 90.

One of the reasons for the inclusion is said to be the elevation of the Union's position in the eyes of God, placing the Union somewhat above that of the Confederacy, thus giving the Union a heavenly advantage. It was, in all senses of the term, propaganda. Then, as now, the thought was not dissimilar to the wanting to raise George Washington to the rank of Saint. How could America be such a great country if not for God's bidding?

In 1907, President Theodore "Teddy" Roosevelt was not pleased with the motto's use on American coinage and paper money. He had the statement removed from the American money, which was not to everyone's liking.

It seemed that one Mr. William Boldly was not happy that the language of God was left off of the new 1907 gold coins and he wrote President Roosevelt to tell him so.

In a letter to Boldly dated November 11 of that year, Roosevelt wrote, "My own feeling in the matter is due to my very firm conviction that to put such a motto (In God We Trust) on coins, or to use it in any kindred manner, not only does no good but does positive harm, and is in effect irreverence, which comes dangerously close to sacrilege..."[8] On November 13, the *New York Times* reported on Roosevelt's comments.[9] A scathing report.

The tone of the column was not because of any dismissal of God by Roosevelt, but of the perceived irreverence by the President. In addition, there was no law requiring such a printing or declaration of the motto "In God We Trust" on any coinage in 1907.

The *Times* also printed the rebuttal by the Episcopal Convention to retain "In God We Trust" on the money. This too was not without heated debate, controversy and, as reported, a certain lack for civility.

It was not until 1955 that "In God We Trust" was ordered by Congress to be placed on our paper money and 1956 "In God We Trust" was made our national motto. Many believe that the reasoning was the Cold War between the United States and the godless communists of the United Soviet Socialist Republic (the former Soviet Union, today's Russia), the People's Republic of China, Cuba and the Eastern European nations. It was a time of the "red scare," Senator Joseph McCarthy's Un-American Activities Committee and a massive buildup of nuclear arms on both sides of Churchill's "Iron Curtain." The question still stands today on whether the Act of Congress in 1956 was part of a greater propaganda scheme. And this leads us to the American Pledge of Allegiance.[10,11]

∽⧼⧽∾

The Pledge of Allegiance

The Pledge of Allegiance has a long history, replete with changes and sidebar stories. In August 1892, Francis Bellamy, a politically socialist minister, wrote what he thought should be the pledge taken by all Americans. The pledge was published that September. In October of that year, on the 400th anniversary of the voyage of Christopher Columbus, the new pledge was recited by over 12 million children across the country.[12]

> "I pledge allegiance to my Flag and the Republic for which it stands, one nation, indivisible, with liberty and justice for all."

It is as important to note what is not said here. "God" is not a part of the original Pledge of Allegiance. Was it because Bellamy was a Socialist? Most likely not; there is no reason why a socialist cannot also be a Christian, Jew or Muslim. There is no indication as to why he chose his words as he did. Socialism in the 1890s had a different meaning than it did in the 1950s and 60s, than it has today, and a different meaning in Europe than in the United States.

We do know that the one of the ideas behind the writing of the Pledge was as a promotion to sell American Flags. Advertising.

In 2008, Shelley Lapkoff, Ph.D., spoke to the Commonwealth Club of California concerning the Pledge that was broadcast live on Minnesota Public Radio. Her conversation concerning Bellamy and Christian Socialism was quite fascinating and insightful.[13] Her presentation provided the verification of the research for much of this section.

In 1923, the language was changed from "my Flag" to "the Flag of the United States of America."

"Under God" was added by President Dwight D. Eisenhower in 1954. He said, "In this way we are reaffirming the transcendence of religious faith in America's heritage and future; *in this way we shall constantly strengthen those spiritual weapons which forever will be our country's most powerful resource in peace and war.*"[14] (Italics added)

Once again, it appears that God was added as a propaganda ploy as America battled those "godless commies."

Propaganda is defined by the *Merriam Webster's Dictionary* as "the spreading of ideas, information, or rumor for the purpose of helping or injuring an institution, a cause, or a person." To cause such an action, the message should be significantly emotional and usually short on solid facts to achieve its goals. By the 1950s, religion had again become a factor in American politics and homes via radio and the new media of television.

The message of the "godless commies" had been prevalent long before the 1917 Russian Revolution and the "loss of religion" in the new Soviet Union was well known to all Americans. Decades later and despite the United States experiencing great prosperity after WW II and the Korean War, there was still an overriding fear of Soviet world domination.

Along with senators Joe McCarthy, Barry Goldwater, and then Vice President Richard M. Nixon, clergy started taking advantage of the anti-communist and conservative sentiment in the United States. The most notable was Fulton Sheen, Archbishop Bishop of the Archdiocese of New York. Sheen hosted the radio show *Catholic Hour* from 1930 until 1950 when he changed to the new media, television, preaching on his new show *Life is Worth Living* and later the *Fulton Sheen Show* until 1968.

Watch the Archbishop on YouTube and you will hear one prevailing message – Communists are atheists and atheists are evil. In a country where every sect of Christianity, as well as Judaism and Islam, are permitted to worship freely, this message from Sheen and other televangelists over the last nine decades still strikes a deep chord of concern.

The Pledge controversy reared its head once more during the June 2011 United States Golf Association's U.S. Open Champion. NBC, the official broadcaster and partner with The Golf Channel, created a very strong and patriotic opening for what many consider one of the two most prestigious golf tournaments. The other is the British Open.

NBC began its coverage on Sunday June 19 with a video showing patriotic scenes and audio included children reciting the Pledge of Allegiance, but not the entire pledge. With some editing, the Pledge heard in this otherwise wonderful opening left out five important words; "...one nation, under God, indivisible..." The reaction was immediate. Internet posts, YouTube videos, blogs, newspapers, magazines, radio and television talking head shows seem to latch on to the "error." But not to all five words missing, but only two, "under God."

The firestorm was immense but short lived, with NBC's Christopher McCloskey, Vice President, Communications for NBC Universal Sports & Olympics, immediately apologizing. "Regrettably, a portion of the Pledge of Allegiance that was in that feature was edited out. It was not done to upset anyone and we'd like to apologize to those of you who were offended by it."[15]

NBC has since removed as many of the videos from the Internet as possible, but rest assure that it will show up again in the near future.

By including "In God We Trust" on our currency for the world to see and "Under God" in the citizen's pledge to the nation for the world to hear, our government unwittingly but successfully amplified the emotional issue of religion and God intertwined with government in the Cold War dialogue.

This knowledge may be disconcerting to many. As one college

administrator told me, "I really don't want God to be used as propaganda."

⋘⋙

Gettysburg Address

We need to back up a bit and return to the American Civil War. Of all the great battles of the war, none was more deadly, none was more devastating, and none was more of a "turning point" than the battle of Gettysburg.[16] Many cite the last sentence in Lincoln's Gettysburg Address as proof that even Lincoln believed the United States was a Christian nation.

> --that this nation, under God, shall have a new birth of freedom--and that government of the people, by the people, for the people, shall not perish from the earth.

Lincoln's attitude towards the breakaway southern states was not "us versus them" but a more parental desire to bring the "children back into the fold." A careful reading of this great speech shows no acknowledgement of the separation of the Union or even recognition of the Confederacy. Lincoln never saw the South as the enemy. There are numerous stories of Lincoln standing at the banks of the Potomac River looking south, not at the enemy but towards a wayward family.

The Gettysburg Address is a eulogy to honor all that battle's 51,000 casualties of which approximately 10,000 died; Union and Confederate soldiers alike.

Contrary to popular myth, Lincoln did not write the Gettysburg Address on the train traveling from Washington, D.C. It started many months earlier with the original drafts written in the White House.

Lincoln had been invited to deliver a few "appropriate remarks" at the dedication of the Gettysburg Cemetery. Yet Lincoln was not the primary speaker at the event; that was to be Edward Everett.[17]

Everett was a former U.S. Senator, Secretary of State, president of Harvard College (University) and a highly respected Unitarian minister. In his two-hours of oratory during the dedication of the new military cemetery, Everett mentioned God only four times, none of which was significant enough to warrant attention.[18]

Lincoln followed Everett with his 273 word dedication, which took about two-minutes to recite. So impressed with the President's words, Everett would later write to Lincoln, "Permit me also to express my great admiration of the thoughts expressed by you, with such eloquent simplicity & appropriateness, at the consecration of the Cemetery. I should be glad, if I could flatter myself that I came as near to the central idea of the occasion, in two hours, as you did in two minutes."[19]

There are five surviving copies of the Address, two at the Library of Congress, one displayed in the White House's Lincoln Room, one at Cornell University (the "Bancroft Copy"), and the last at the Illinois State Historical Library (the "Everett Copy").[20] Of these, the two at the LOC, known as the "Nicolay" and the "Hay" copies, do not have "Under God" written into the drafts.

It must be noted that only the Nicolay copy was written on White House letterhead. Because of the official paper, the Nicolay copy is also known as the "first draft."

The draft hung in the White House is the only one dated, so there are no additional clues to the order of the five copies.[21, 22]

The copy in the White House, known as the "Bliss Copy," was dated and signed by the President on November 19, 1863. It is also the only copy with the lead comment, "Address delivered at the dedication of the Cemetery at Gettysburg." However, the question remains if this was the version that Lincoln in fact read.

How "under God" arrived in the Address is a great mystery and the rumors seem to have proliferated since the development of Internet conspiracy sites. There appear to be significant proofs available from newspaper reports of the time that Lincoln did say "under God," though skeptics like James Randi, co-founder of the Center of Inquiry, believes otherwise.

Some believe that Lincoln added the words at the last moment. Still others believe that a minister from a Gettysburg church, who was invited to have dinner with the dignitaries the night before, had asked Lincoln to include the phrase. None can be substantiated.

The Gettysburg Address's "controversy" is still alive and well in the 21st century and can only be chalked up to cultural and religious battles in the United States. One such battle was initiated by Bob Unruh writing for WorldNetDaily.com claiming that God has been dropped from the Gettysburg Address.[23] Mr. Unruh relied solely on a July 2010 blog article written by Robert George for the e-zine "First Things."[24] George based his complaint on a pamphlet printed and distributed earlier that month.

The pamphlet in question, titled "The Declaration of Independence, The Gettysburg Address and The Constitution," was printed by the American Constitution Society for Law and Policy.[25] ACS's mission is to promote "the vitality of the U.S. Constitution and the fundamental values: individual rights and liberties it expresses, genuine equality, access to justice, democracy and the rule of law."

On page 9 of the pamphlet, in a section titled the "Pocket Constitution," is the Gettysburg Address printed without the words "under God."[26] The Pamphlet also describes the draft printed as the "Hay Copy" which, as noted above, does not include "under God." It is important to note that neither George nor Unruh refer to the multiple drafts of the Address, only to the apparent deletion of the two words, "under God." It is quite unfortunate that the George and Unruh commentaries were reprinted verbatim and cited on so many web sites without any investigation.[27]

With basic research, it is found that 1) the Hay Copy does not and never did contain the words "under God," 2)the Gettysburg Address was never "sanitized" of God, and 3) both primary conspiracy writers and those who reprinted their work, failed to conduct due diligence.

ಆಣಿಶಿಖ

Conclusion

Though many attempts have been made to correlate these American documents and mottos, the anthem and the pledge as being proof of Christian nation status, the proponents' proofs fall short. The arguments fail to meet the tests of proof, mostly due to the lack of supporting evidence. The Constitution and Articles were not dedicated to a supreme deity. God was added to our motto and coinage as a propaganda ploy, and the controversies over Lincoln's address had too many holes to be titled a "proof."

As mentioned, it also appears that those who are promulgating at least these Christian nation proofs have not done the research to determine if the proofs are correct. It is this lack of due diligence that is creating many of the conflicts concerning the discussion.

Chapter 11

The Court Cases

ଔଅଔଅ

When it comes to judicial case law, objective proofs provided by the Christian nation proponents center on three United States Supreme Court decisions. A fourth court case is also cited; however, it concerned the New York State law and was heard in the New York courts only.

Many historians have noted that the Founders did not want an efficient government; they wanted a safe government, thus built in the series of checks and balances. The court is the third level of these checks, with oversight of the executive and legislative branches. The court's job, for the purpose of this discussion, is twofold. The first is to interpret the laws as written by Congress and approved by the President. The second is to tell the Congress and the President when they have written a statute or made an order that the court believes may be in violation of the Constitution's mandate.

Some argue that Justice John Marshall established type of "judicial review" of constitutional law in Mulbury v. Madison.[1] This may not be wholly correct. Article III, Section 2, clause 1 of the Constitution states that, "The judicial Power shall extend to all Cases, in Law and Equity, arising under this Constitution, the Laws of the United States, and Treaties made, or which shall be made, under their Authority." This clause appears to grant the Court the authority of judicial review, but the young nation and its courts had not yet taken on this issue.

Regardless of claims to the contrary, the court does not make law, but makes the rulings on how the law is to be interpreted by lower courts and by enforcement officials. Statutes are, therefore, written specifically vague - specific enough to know what the rules are, but vague enough to allow the rule to be interpreted or modified to the situation and time may demand. The three level of judicial oversight, district, Appeals and Supreme, are the internal check of the rulings and decisions.

Most Christian nation proponents claim that each of the four court cases provides precedents and proofs for the Christian nation position. There is, unfortunately, one caveat; precedent is usually set by the court's decision, not by the testimony used during the court's debate. Even then, the Supreme Court may, has, and still declares certain decisions to be limited to the single case argued and not as precedent to all cases.

The four cases, though involving religion, were not brought based on a religious precursor. As we shall see, the cases are as diverse as the religions in this country. The quotes for each case are meant to show the religious aspects of the cases.

Please note that cases concerning prayer in school, nativity scenes, the Ten Commandments in classrooms or courthouses, were not brought up by the defenders of the Christian nation theories, therefore are not discussed here. The proponents did not bring these cases up because, for the most part, they were heard in favor of "separation."

CHURCH OF THE HOLY TRINITY V. US (1892) *"No purpose of action against any religion can be imputed to any legislation, State or national, because this is a religious people... this is a Christian nation."*

Holy Trinity v. US (143 U.S. 457)[2] dealt with a very interesting issue, whether a contract between a religious society incorporated in the United States and a citizen of another country was legal under "The Act of February 26, 1880."

The statute was designed "to prohibit the importation and migration of foreigners and aliens under contract or agreement to perform labor in the United States, its Territories, and the District of Columbia."[3, 4] This case argued the legal dilemma whether a church in New York could contract with a minister in England to bring that minister to New York to perform his duties.

In reading the basis of the legal action, it appears that this case could have been brought to the court whether or not a religious society was involved. It is by the situation, not the affiliation, which this case just happens to involve a Christian church. The contract could have been with a haberdasher, a blacksmith with specific skills, or an artisan skilled in making wooden furniture. The contracting organization could have been a town, school, or private business. It was just happenstance that in this case a church was contracting a new minister from England.

Religion became a centering point of *Holy Trinity v. US* only in the arguments, but is taken by the some proponents of the Christian nation theories as a major proof. The court's decision talks only in terms of whether the religious order's contract was within or outside the scope of the law. The court, in its deliberation, said "beyond all these matters, no purpose of action against religion can be imputed to any legislation, state or national, because this is a religious people." (143 U. S. 465) The court specifically talked to the Church of the Holy Trinity and not the people of the nation. This appears to be an acknowledgement not of the Christian faith, per se, but of the general religiosity of the nation, be it Christian, Jewish or otherwise.

Associate Justice David Brewer, writing for the majority, stated that the religious confluences of the nation, including dedicating an oath in God's name, the opening of deliberative sessions with prayer and so on, should,

> ...add a volume of *unofficial declarations to the mass of organic utterances that this is a Christian nation*. In the face of all these, shall it be believed that a Congress of the United States intended to make it a misdemeanor for a church of this country to contract for the services of a Christian minister residing in another nation?" (143 U.S. 471) (Italic added)

The statement is part of a question, not the utterance of a statement of a national religious fervor. Justice Brewer did not end his ruling there. The quote starting this section was not part of the ruling, only a direction Brewer appeared to take towards his conclusion. He continued,

> If we examine the constitutions of the various states, we find in them a constant recognition of religious obligations. Every Constitution of every one of the forty-four states contains language which, either directly or by clear implication, recognizes a profound reverence for religion, and an assumption that its influence in all human affairs is essential to the wellbeing of the community." (147 U.S. 468)

This is not a declaration that we are a Christian nation, but that the United States is a nation where the multitude of beliefs has a collective influence on its citizen's daily lives and as an affirmation of the First Amendment.

Justice Brewer concluded reminding the court that the statute argued was not designed for a specific "evil" but was written so broadly in scope that it could not be enforced without being injurious to many communities, including the religious communities, of the United States. Justice Brewer stated that if a proposed law specifically mentioning the hiring of religious leaders from overseas to preach to Roman Catholic, Episcopal, Baptist and Jewish congregations were to be put in front of Congress, it would never be passed.

Brewer concluded,

> It is the duty of the courts under those circumstances to say that, however broad the language of the statute may be, the act, although within the letter, is not within the intention of the legislature, and therefore cannot be within the statute.
>
> The judgment will be reversed, and the case remanded for further proceedings in accordance with this opinion.

This ruling came from the belief that the government should neither hinder nor support religious activities. In this case, it appeared to the court that there was an undue hindrance by the law concerning the Free Expression clause of the Constitution.

When this case was argued, the religious sanctions by individual states had already been challenged. The Fourteenth Amendment protected the rights dictated by the Constitution and its Amendments from abridgment by state leaders and governments.

The First Amendment's sanction of religious freedoms was not intensely argued until 1947 in *Everson v. Board of Education of Ewing*

Township (NJ), 330 U.S. 1(1947). This case concerned the district allowing "the reimbursement of schools for the transportation of students to private schools."[5] This and following cases did not discuss the religiosity of the nation but were defining the question as to the line of separation.

Finding in the Board's favor, the court decided that as long as the moneys did not flow directly to the church-sanctioned schools but was used as it would be used for public institutions for the transportation of students, the practice was acceptable.

It is unfortunate that those who represented these two cases as supporting their views that the United States is a Christian nation misrepresent the text of the rulings. The two statements provided by the proponents are a strange mix and out of context with the ruling. The first does not follow the second, in paragraph or page. There is a large section of the ruling that is conveniently left out.

In this case, as a commentary, I cannot say the quote opening this section is precise or a proof of the religion of this nation. The opening quote is not accurate either in context or in its interpretation by the Christian nation proponents. The statement read in full and in context says that the idea that a church is involved is not the issue and any restriction of church activities by the state or federal goivernments is prohibited by the Constitution (with some exception as the courts will later define). The issue was in fact and issue of contract law and whether that law restricted the practice of one's faith. In this case, the answer was "yes." It was not, however, a declaration of a national religion.

THE PEOPLE V. RUGGLES (1811) - *We are a Christian people and the morality of the country is deeply engrafted upon Christianity and not upon the doctrines or worship of those impostors* [other religions].

The basis of *People v. Ruggles* is not one of religion, but one of free speech.[6] The case dealt with New York State law, not federal, and was heard in the New York courts, not federal; therefore it does not have relevance outside of the state of New York except as an excellent example of the court's ability to separate sectarian and secular laws. In case law, this case is referred to as *8 Johns R. 290 NY*. There are no references to this case in the federal court system.

According to the summary provided by the University of Chicago, the argument was not whether the United States is a Christian nation, but "the object [of this case was] the 38th article of the [New York] constitution... to 'guard against spiritual oppression and intolerance,' by declaring that 'the free exercise and enjoyment of religious profession and worship, without discrimination or preference, should forever thereafter be allowed within this state, to all mankind.' "

The charge was that the defendant did,

> ...wickedly, maliciously, and blasphemously utter, in the presence and hearing of divers good and christian people, these false, feigned, scandalous, malicious, wicked and blasphemous words, to wit, '*Jesus Christ was a bastard, and his mother must be a whore;*' and the single question is, whether this be a public offence by the law of the land. After conviction, we must intend that these words were uttered in a wanton manner, and, as they evidently import, with a wicked and malicious disposition, and not in a serious discussion upon any controverted point in religion.

This appears to follow the intent of the First Amendment's

purposeful connection between the freedom to practice ones' religion and the freedom of speech. This also appears to determine, at least in part and for the State of New York, where the idea of free expression becomes primary and adds to that a restriction as to when speech is used to purposely harm another.

By 1811, New York State no longer had an "official" church, which would indicate that Christianity was not a prerequisite for a civil society. However, the case appears to deal with language and statements that may appear as blasphemies to one or many segments of the community at large and, therefore, malicious. In short, this had more to do with the act of civil disobedience against the church than about religion itself. It is indeed true that the majority of residents in New York City, where the case originated, were Christians by virtue of their ancestral homelands in Europe; it was the verbal attack on a religious belief that caused the action, not the keeping of religious ideals.

The case dealt with "common law" as much as it did with Article 38 of the New York State Constitution. Kent wrote,

> The free, equal, and undisturbed, enjoyment of religious opinion, whatever it may be, and free and decent discussions on any religious subject, is granted and secured; but to revile, with malicious and blasphemous contempt, the religion professed by almost the whole community, is an abuse of that right. Nor are we bound, by any expressions in the constitution, as some have strangely supposed, either not to punish at all, or to punish indiscriminately the like attacks upon the religion of *Mahomet*or of the grand *Lama;* and for this plain reason, that the case assumes that we are a christian people, and the

morality of the country is deeply ingrafted *[sic]* upon christianity, and not upon the doctrines or worship of those impostors.

In other words, it did not matter what religion one professed, the idea of such language clearly demonstrated malice towards those who accepted that faith and was designed to injure those parties.

Kent's statement would indicate that disagreements and discussions were not only permitted but encouraged under the laws of the state, that state's constitution and the United States Constitution. However, name-calling when designed to injure or harm an individual or group of people because of their beliefs was not and would not be tolerated by New York State.

The summary's concluding statement says, "Surely, then, we are bound to conclude, that wicked and malicious words, writings and actions which go to vilify those gospels, continue, as at common law, to be an offence against the public peace and safety. They are inconsistent with the reverence due to the administration of an oath, and among their other evil consequences, they tend to lessen, in the public mind, its religious sanction."

As for the quote itself at the beginning of this section, it does not appear in the summary sited above. After a conversation with the Hofstra University Law Library, a full copy of the court's decision was obtained and reviewed.

The defense argued,

> ...that the offence state charged in the indictment was not punishable by the law of this state [New York], though, he admitted, it was punishable by the common law of England, where Christianity makes part of the law of the land. From the preamble, and the provisions

of the constitution of this state, and the silence of the legislature, it was inferred that Christianity was not a part of the common law of this state. There are no statutes concerning religion, except this state those relative to the Sabbath, and to suppress immorality. The constitution allows a free toleration to all religions and all kinds of worship. It is not an offence against religion in general; nor does it affect moral evidence, or destroy confidence in human testimony.[7]

The decision was that of the New York State Supreme Court, New York's sole court of the time, not the United States Supreme Court. The court's opinion, therefore, was applicable to New York, but not U.S. wide. This, unfortunately, is misstated as a United States Supreme Court case in a number of web sites, leading readers to a false claim.

What is important is that the basis of many of the current court cases concerning religion and government comes from the ideal of Ruggles. Many of the lawsuits now facing the various courts are based on the third portion of the First Amendment, the freedom of expression. Westboro Baptist Church is allowed, within reason, to protest at the funerals of our military men and women who died in battle, not because they are Christians (which is highly questioned by many) but because the Constitution says they can. As can neo-Nazis, skinheads, racist minority groups, and those who do not want a mosque, temple or church in their neighborhood.

෴

VIDAL VS. GIRARD'S EXECUTORS (1844) - It is unnecessary for us, however, to consider the establishment of a school or college for the propagation of Judaism or Deism or any other form of infidelity. Such a case is not to be presumed to exist in a Christian country.

This is United States Supreme Court case 43U.S.127 2HOW.127

11L.ED.205 involving a will that provided $2,000,000 to the city of Philadelphia to build a "college."[8] It was, in fact, a school for young orphan boys. It is important to note here the parties involved in this case, the family of the deceased, Stephen Girard, versus the executor of the will, designated as the mayor and citizens of Philadelphia.

Mr. Girard immigrated to the United States from his native France in the early 1770s, "shortly before the [United States'] declaration of independence." Girard had been a resident of Philadelphia from about 1781 until his death in 1831, becoming a wealthy man. In his will, which is noted in the opinion along with its addendums, Girard left $2 million to build and support a school for "poor male white orphan children" ages 6 to 10, stating that the city and its government be the executor of the will and responsible for the construction and operations of the "new college." Mr. Girard evidently believed that American blacks did not deserve an education though "the law of 1780 which abolished slavery in Pennsylvania actually had more immediate impact on the free blacks than the enslaved ones. The abolition of slavery was very gradual, while the restrictive laws on free blacks were lifted at once."[9]

The will documented the subject matter to be taught and "barred clergymen of any denomination from holding any post within the college and from visiting the premises." It was to this provision the family in France took exception and filed suit.[10]

In addition to the school, Girard also provided moneys to the state of Pennsylvania for canal improvements, and $500,000 to the city of Philadelphia for road and lighting improvements. Girard's heart was in the right place when it came to his adopted state and city, except for the black community.

The quote above provided as "proof" by proponents is part of the argument and testimony, not the opinion of the court. The family believed that Girard's will violated Pennsylvania's common laws and practice by prohibiting religious personnel of any sect to have access to the school and the teaching of ethics as a secular concept instead of a religious ideal.

The court stated in the paragraph prior to the quote,

> ... no man can of right be compelled to attend, erect, or support any place of worship, or to maintain any ministry against his consent; no human authority can, in any case whatever, control or interfere with the rights of conscience; and no preference shall ever be given by law to any religious establishment or modes of worship.' Language more comprehensive for the complete protection of every variety of religious opinion could scarcely be used; and it must have been intended to extend equally to all sects, whether they believed in Christianity or not, and whether they were Jews or infidels.[11]

This statement appears to declare that Pennsylvania, at least, did not construct Christianity in any form as the sole religion of the state. It may also suggested that even if one were a deist, agnostic, atheist or any one of the Eastern religions, individual faith or lack of was acceptable to the state.

The court's decision was based on the principle that Girard "wanted the students to remain free from sectarian controversy and wished them to study a curriculum that did not place inordinate emphasis on religious subjects. He did not proscribe members of the laity from teaching the general principles of Christianity or analyzing the Bible from a historical perspective."[12]

The court's conclusion:

> Looking to the objection therefore in a mere juridical

view, which is the only one in which we are at liberty to consider it, we are satisfied that there is nothing in the devise establishing the college, or in the regulations and restrictions contained therein, which are inconsistent with the Christian religion, or are opposed to any known policy of the state of Pennsylvania.

This reading renders it unnecessary for us to examine the other and remaining question, to whom, if the will were void, the property would belong, whether it would fall into the residue of the estate devised to the city, or become a resulting trust for the heirs at law.

Though this may be considered a test of Christianity's role in America, it was not. It was, however, a test of a common practice of requiring religion to be taught in a private school, whether the prohibiting of any ministers (Christian, Jewish, Muslim or otherwise), or whether the city of Philadelphia had the right to be the executor of the will of Stephen Girard was contrary to state, federal or common law. It is not a test of whether the United States is a Christian nation.

As with the previous argument, the quote appears taken out of context and without consideration of the entire opinion.

03808003

UNITED STATES V. MACINTOSH, 283 U.S. 605 (1931) - We are a Christian people ... according to one another the equal right of religious freedom and acknowledging with reverence the duty of obedience to the will of God.

This case concerned religious freedom, but not whether the United States is a Christian nation in terms of law or Constitution. The problem here deals with the oath of naturalization and the morality of war.

Mr. Macintosh, a Canadian citizen, wished to become a naturalized

U.S. citizen, but he refused to pledge to take up arms in defense of his new country. He would only fight for his country if he thought the war was morally justified. On his citizenship application he wrote,

> I am willing to do what I judge to be in the best interests of my country, but only in so far as I can believe that this is *not going to be against the best interests of humanity* in the long run. I do not undertake to support 'my country, right or wrong' in any dispute which may arise, and I am not willing to promise beforehand, and without knowing the cause for which my country may go to war, either that I will or that I will not 'take up arms in defense of this country,' however 'necessary' the war may seem to be to the Government of the day.[13] (Italics added)

While Macintosh was willing to give allegiance to the United States, he was not willing to put country ahead of his allegiance to humanity.[14]

Mr. Macintosh's argument was simple, how can anyone else, especially a government, make his moral decisions? His moral principles, he believed, were based on Christian and humanistic morals as he understood them. However, the case only dealt with whether Macintosh was permitted to decide for himself if a war was moral under his own methods of declaration for the entire nation.

The testimony in Macintosh continued:

> But, also, we are a nation with the duty to survive; a nation whose Constitution contemplates war as well as peace; whose government must go forward upon the assumption, and safely can proceed upon no other, that unqualified allegiance to the nation and submission and obedience to the laws of the land, as well those

made for war as those made for peace, are not inconsistent with the will of God.

As with the cases already cited, the quote was part of the argument and not part of the decision of the case. In addition, the quote given as argument was originally found in *Holy Trinity v. U.S.*

The court's finding was against Mr. Macintosh, not based on his religious beliefs, but on his conscientious objector morals.

The Naturalization Act is to be construed "with definite purpose to favor and support the government," and the United States is entitled to the benefit of any doubt which remains in the mind of the court as to any essential matter of fact. The burden was upon the applicant to show that his views were not opposed to the Constitution but only to war.

> "The principle that it is a duty of citizenship by force of arms when necessary to defend the country against all enemies, and that [his] opinions and beliefs would not prevent or impair the true faith and allegiance required by the act." *United States v. Schwimmer, supra,* 279 U. S. 649-650, 279 U. S. 653.

The decision in Macintoch was based on the Schwimmer test.

> We are of opinion that he did not meet this requirement. The examiner and the court of first instance who heard and weighed the evidence and saw the applicant and witnesses so concluded. That conclusion, if we were in doubt, would not be rejected except for good and persuasive reasons, which we are unable to find.

> The decree of the court of appeals is reversed, and that of the district court is affirmed.

I am afraid that Mr. Macintosh was not granted citizenship.

However, the ruling was reversed and the Schwimmer test abandoned by the Supreme Court with a change in law in 1941 allowing for the conscientious objector status.

Once again, the proponents of the Christian nation position have seemingly taken the quote out of context and failed to review the entire case or print the entire section and, thusly, the quote does not justify the proponent's position of Christian nation status.

Other Cases

The court cases concerning religion and government did not stop in 1931 and continue to this date. Many decisions, like the 1961 U.S. Supreme court case of *Torcaso v. Watkins*, 367 U.S. 488 (1961), were based on whether the state can require a belief in God as a qualifier for a government appointed or elected official.[15]

More specifically, this case surrounded the idea that a person who is an atheist could not hold an office of public responsibility in Maryland. "Torcaso was appointed to the office of Notary Public by the Governor of Maryland, but was refused a commission to serve because he would not declare his belief in God."[16]

Writing for the majority, Justice Hugo Black wrote, "The power and authority of the State of Maryland thus is put on the side of one particular sort of believers -- those who are willing to say they believe in 'the existence of God.' " Though there was noted precedent for this for such a law prior to 1789, Black quoted another Supreme Court case while working towards the opinion of the court.

> We decided [in] *Everson v. Board of Education,* 330 U. S. 1, and said this at pages 330 U. S. 15 and 330 U. S. 16:

> "The 'establishment of religion' clause of the First Amendment means at least this: neither a state nor the Federal Government can set up a church. Neither can pass laws which aid one religion, aid all religions, or prefer one religion over another. Neither can force nor influence a person to go to or to remain away from church against his will or force him to profess a belief or disbelief in any religion. No person can be punished for entertaining or professing religious beliefs or disbeliefs, for church attendance or nonattendance. No tax in any amount, large or small, can be levied to support any religious activities or institutions, whatever they may be called, or whatever form they may adopt to teach or practice religion. Neither a state nor the Federal Government can, openly or secretly, participate in the affairs of any religious organizations or groups, and vice versa. In the words of Jefferson, the clause against establishment of religion by law was intended to erect 'a wall of separation between church and State.'"

The Court found for Torcaso.

> We repeat and again reaffirm that neither a State nor the Federal Government can constitutionally force a person "to profess a belief or disbelief in any religion." Neither can constitutionally pass laws or impose requirements which aid all religions as against nonbelievers, and neither can aid those religions based on a belief in the existence of God as against those religions founded on different beliefs.
>
> Such laws and state constitutional provisions, such as

North Carolina's Article VI, Section 8 were not only in violation of the United States Constitution Article VI, clause 3 disallowing any religious test to hold office, but the First and Fourteenth Amendments. North Caroline disqualified, "any person who shall deny the being of Almighty God."[17]

In all, there is more evidence that the Constitution, thus the founding of the nation, was secular, pluralistic and not based on Christian beliefs or any one denomination or sect. The rights of all those who do not believe in any of the Christian faiths needed to be honored as those who are Christians.

Today, however, that sentiment has gone further to an accusatory level. So-called wars on Christianity and on Christmas have been claimed by many, though there is no evidence of such conflicts.[18]

ଔଈଓଈଓ

The Wars Against Christianity

David Limbaugh's *Persecution: How Liberals are Waging War on Christianity* specifically pits one political school against the other, liberals versus conservatives.[19] Limbaugh's approach would lead one to believe that this is a great and unrelenting "war" between Christians and atheists.

Part II, "War for the Public Square," contains many an anecdote concerning his position, and even without examining each case, they seem implausible or in some cases simply absurd. On the surface at least, Limbaugh appears to at least suggest denying the rights of people who are not Christians, thus extending any "war" from their own trenches. By blaming the liberal political faction for all that ails, Limbaugh and other supporters of the war against Christianity theories are saying they are Christian conservatives and everyone hates them because of their theocratic politics. There is some evidence to support this claim, but no compelling evidence.

However, the courts have also found in favor of religious organizations, Christian and otherwise, something the Christian nation proponents fails to recognize. Like *Everson v. Board of Education*, there are cases noted by the University of Virginia School of Law that support some state involvement in religious activities.

In *Mueller v. Allen*, 463 U.S. 388 (1983) the Supreme Court, in a 5-4 vote, allowed tax deductions to be made by parents with students attending religious schools.[20]

"The Court upheld the Louisiana statute that provided state funds for the purchasing of textbooks for both religious and public school students," in *Cochran v. Louisiana*, 281 U.S. 370.[21]

In *Board of Education of the Westside Community Schools v. Mergens* (496 U.S. 226 (1990)), the courts sided with students who wanted to start a "Christian Club" in their high school. Writing for the majority, Justice Sandra Day O'Conner said that because officials would have little or no role in the group's activities, such a ban would violate the group's right to equal access and the students were mature enough to recognize that allowing a religious club did not constitute a sanction of religion by the school board.

Justice Kennedy, writing for the majority in *Rosenberger v. Rector and Visitors of the University of Virginia* (515 U.S. 819 (1995)), said that the University of Virginia could not deny a campus-based organization the funds to print "Wide Awake: A Christian Perspective at the University of Virginia" because the University's rules did not prevented in the past religious themes in printed material. It must be noted here that the university also provided moneys to secular recognized groups.

One argument against the Christian nation theory is found in *West Virginia State Board of Education v. Barnette*. In his ruling, Justice Robert H. Jackson stated, "There is no mysticism in the American concept of the State or of the nature or origin of its authority. We set up government by consent of the governed, and the Bill of Rights denies those in power any legal opportunity to coerce that consent."[22]

West Virginia State Board of Education v. Bernette, 319 U.S. 624 (1943), 319 U.S. 624, involved a previous Supreme Court ruling in *Minersville School District v. Gobitis*, 310 U.S. 586 , 60 S.Ct. 1010, 127 A.L.R. 1493 in which siblings Lillian and William refused to say the Pledge of Alliance in school.[23] Their reason for refusal was religious based; their family was Jehovah's Witnesses and the taking of oath was contrary to their interpretation of scripture. The question before the court concerning *Gobitis* was a First Amendment rights case affecting the Free Exercise and Free Expression clauses.

The rule issued by the Pennsylvania school district stated "that all teachers and pupils shall be required to participate in the salute honoring the Nation represented by the Flag; provided, however, that refusal to salute the Flag be regarded as an Act of insubordination, and shall be dealt with accordingly."[24] There were no exceptions made for religious or conscientious objections to the rule.

Associate Justice Felix Frankfurter wrote for the majority saying that the institutions of family and religious freedom were paramount to and honored the concepts of which the flag is a symbol.

> A society which is dedicated to the preservation of these ultimate values of civilization may in self-protection utilize the educational process for inculcating those almost unconscious feelings which bind men together in a comprehending loyalty, whatever may be their lesser differences and difficulties. That is to say, the

process may be utilized so long as men's right to believe as they please, to win others to their way of belief, and their right to assemble in their chosen places of worship for the devotional ceremonies of their faith, are all fully respected.

Conscientious scruples have not, in the course of the long struggle for religious toleration, relieved the individual from obedience to a general law not aimed at the promotion or restriction of religious beliefs. The mere possession of religious convictions which contradict the relevant concerns of a political society does not relieve the citizen from the discharge of political responsibilities.[25]

The Court found in favor of Lillian and William.

A similar issue was taken up by the court in 1943. In attempting to comply with *Gobitis*, the West Virginia State Board of Education attempted to rewrite their rules for reciting the Pledge. West Virginia's rule stated that American history and civics "courses of instruction in history, civics, and in the Constitutions of the United States and of the State 'for the purpose of teaching, fostering and perpetuating the ideals, principles and spirit of Americanism, and increasing the knowledge of the organization and machinery of the government.' The Board of Education's rules continued that each teacher and student would use a commonly accepted salute to the Flag." That salute was defined as an outstretched right arm, palm up.

There were two complaints. First was the salute itself. In 1943, the United States and Allied forces were well into the war against the Axis powers of Germany, Italy, and Japan. The salute required was initially a stiff arm salute, similar as the salute of the Nazi party and Hitler, but with right palm up. That rule was later modified to be simply holding the right palm up and saying the pledge without the "stiff arm" requirement.

The second major complaint was the matter of the court case; there were no exceptions made for religious or conscientious belief. The Barnette's were also Jehovah Witnesses who took Exodus 20: 4, 5 literally, that they were not to bow down or swear allegiance to any "graven image" of any god or temporal power. This included the flag and the government of the United States. This did not make them bad citizens, but placed their God above all else.

Justice Robert H. Jackson wrote,

> "If there is any fixed star in our constitutional constellation, it is that no official, high or petty, can prescribe what shall be orthodox in politics, nationalism, religion, or other matters of opinion or force citizens to confess by word or act their faith therein. If there are any circumstances which permit an exception, they do not now occur to us."[26]

Over the years, it appears that the United States Supreme Court has been consistent and equally reverent to both sides of the arguments concerning religion and government, whether that is local or federal, school or prayer at work.

In their book, *Religious Freedom and the Constitution*, Christopher Eisgruber and Lawrence Sager argue that this "equal liberty" standard should be the way of the courts, as opposed to the "no hindrance" usually applied.[27] The authors believe that religious institutions have neither special benefits nor special restrictions and must be seen in the same light as any other institution.

This chapter argues that equal liberty was in fact applied to these and other cases, finding for and against religious institution as described in the Constitution's First Amendment, but never denying nor limiting equal status under the eyes of the courts.

In all decisions, whether one agrees or not, it was the reading of the Constitution and the reliance on the temporal laws that maintained our freedom to practice our individual faiths while not being forced to accept any single faith favored by government.

In those decisions quoted by the Christian theories proponents, the language indeed was there, but misappropriated to precedent setting as opposed to witness statements. In the other cases cited, the courts held to the belief that secular and sectarian laws are important, need to be honored but must remain separate partners in our pluralistic republic.

CSEOEOCR

Conclusion

In the four cases referred to by the Christian nation proponents and the quotes from those cases, one must admit that, yes, the quotes do exist. However, these quote were taken out of context, or rearranged, and are not considered "precedent setting" in the eyes of the courts in the United States. They were all part of the evidence provided by the parties involved in the cases.

As for there being a war on Christianity by the atheists, the liberals, the courts and the government, there appears to be no evidence to justify that allegation. In fact, it appears that the courts have ruled for the American religious institutions as it has against them.

It can only be concluded that if such an organized war existed, it must have started with the Ma-re Mount colony, continued through the teachings of Aristotle, Voltaire, Locke and others, and came to a head as the Founders' enlightenment illuminated the problems when church and state do not remain in their own temples.

Chapter 12

In the End

Outside our borders

One of the great curiosities during this exercise was discovering how others see the United States in terms of our Constitution, plurality, and religion. From the "main-stream news," one would suspect that after President George W. Bush's error of saying that our war against the Taliban and al Qaeda was a "crusade," most in the Muslim world would have seen the war as one of religion.

Indeed, many Americans have made that statement in the United States concerning not only Islamic extremists and terrorists, but concerning all Muslims. Protests of Islamic civic centers in New York, Tennessee, California, and elsewhere were used as political gunpowder in the 2010 elections. We are seeing the War on Terrorism, read Muslims, again rearing its head in the 2012 presidential election cycle. In fact, religion has become very prominent one again.

ABC's *20/20* and *This Week with Christiane Amanpour*, as well as PBS's *God In America* asked some stunning questions. How has religious belief shaped American history? What role have religious ideas and spiritual experience played in shaping the social, political, and cultural life of what has become the world's most religiously diverse nation? What is America's "special relationship" with God?

Many have attempted to tackle these questions in the States and overseas. It seems that the more conservative religious communities, Christian, Jewish, and Muslim, remain the loudest of the voices in the sea of religious anger. America's conservative-Christian voices often appear to be the loudest.

Writing to journalists, teachers, and intellectuals around the world, I asked how they viewed the United States, its constitutional guarantees, and of our state of religion. I received answers from Europe, Asia, India and Pakistan, and, of course, the Middle East. The answers were truly a mixed bag. All of these responses came before the 2011 Arab Spring, the series of civil unrest that has lead to regime changes throughout Africa and the Middle East.

Some of the foreign responders believe that the U.S. Constitution prevents the United States from being a Christian country. With the single exception of those Americans on religious missions overseas, religion is rarely an issue concerning American tourists outside of the Middle East. Of course in Israel Christians, Jews, and Muslims pilgrims make their way to holy sites and religion is often the topic of the moment.

Andrew Zimmern, host of the Travel Channel's *Bizarre Foods* said that during his visit to Syria, as a Jew born in New York, it was only when he visited a mosque in Damascus that religion was even broached. Even then, his religion or religious beliefs were never questioned.

One correspondent from Mumbai, India talked about the sensitivity of American tourists and business representatives to the various Indian religions and myths. It is the same throughout the world. Americans are seen as tolerant and accepting of all religions.

Only those in the Muslim communities are much divided on this point. Here, it appears that the teaching of individual mosques has more to do with attitude towards the American government and towards Americans in general, than actual knowledge.

Anne Hunt, political correspondent for Affiliated Press Euro-zone, asked a curious question. With religion taking a back seat in Europe, why have Americans embraced their religion, especially Christianity, so tightly?

⋘⋙

Reaching the Conclusion

Unfortunately, an answer to that and similar questions is not easy to find, and when it does surface, it is rarely agreed upon, and brings us right back state side.

Understanding or believing in the religiosity of America has nothing to do with education, intelligence, critical thinking skills, or economic status. It does involve the stability of the country, prosperity, and if the United States is involved in a war. To attempt to define the ups and downs of American religiosity in more historical terms would most likely require a vast amount of research, justification and verification.

The original colonization of the new continent was for commerce, religion was secondary or tertiary. The Founders, pious and not, Christians, deists and possibly an atheist or two, lived in a period of time when religion and government were heavily intertwined in Europe and by extension in the colonies. The Founders saw the dangers in the continuation of that practice. The facts show that terms such as

"Creator" did not denote a Christian God but a power much greater and more expansive, and not involved in our day-to-day lives but who or which, lit the match for the Big Bang.

A number of our Founders, including Washington, Jefferson, Franklin and Madison, not only accepted the multitude of Christian sects, but they understood that a great society must include Jews, Muslims, atheists, deists and others. The documents show this wanting of a secular government that recognizes the religions of man; that did not want to either impose faith or deny one's beliefs. There are no proofs otherwise.

The evidence shows the misquoting of United States and New York court cases in the hopes of supporting the proponents' position. The evidence also shows a lack of due diligence in research on the part of the proponents and, therefore, misinterpretation. This is extended to the due diligence of the readers of and those who redistribute misinformation as "truth."

Is the misquoting and misinterpretations done purposely? I truly doubt that. I believe it is a matter of what is learned and reinforced as we grow up in this society of free thought and free religious practices.

Most important, the evidence points to a much bigger problem, the lost competency of critical thinking and due diligent research. This statement may be insulting to some readers, but there will be no apology. Reading anything as absolute, including this book, is wrong. That includes reading the various bibles or other holy writings not just as truth, but the absolute truth. Acceptance without investigation is as dangerous as opinion without evidence, and is used to the advantage by propagandists offering emotional proofs with nothing solid to back up their claims.

Maybe Geoff Crocker had the right idea (though misdirected) in his book *An Enlightened Philosophy: Can an atheist believe anything?*

Crocker premise is that atheists need to look at the great holy stories as myths and look towards the meaning of the parables. By doing this, Crocker suggests, we would live in a much better world.

In fact, atheists do read the holy books as myths and only myths. It may be the newest branch of Puritanism made up of those believing in the infallibility of the Christian Bible (which includes the Torah) is growing faster than expected and that critical thinking and listening skills are being lost to absolutism.

In his evidence, Crocker's attempts to prove his position may have proven just the opposite - that if those of religion could see their stories as myths, maybe the world would be better.[1]

A September 2010 Pew Charitable Trust poll indicated that atheists and agnostics had a better grasp of "religious knowledge" than evangelical and fundamentalist Christians when it came to knowledge of the biblical teachings and history.[2] American non-Christians as a whole seem to have a better grasp of other world religions, including Islam, than their more orthodox Christian brethren. Most interesting is that atheists, agnostics, and Jews knew more about what the Constitution says about religion than Christians.

The United States was not founded as a Christian nation. America may currently be more religious than any other modern country, but in fact American Christians do not agree which bible is the right bible, which interpretations of the texts are the right interpretations, or even, on the question tackled here, whether or not the United States was founded as a Christian nation.

Then there is the question of whether Christian, Jews, Muslims and others are growing in numbers, or if more men and women are turning to deism, agnosticism, or atheism as their core "belief system."

The old adage that "numbers don't lie, but liars use numbers" holds for evidence as well. Do not take this book sitting down; do not agree or disagree without examining what has been said in these pages. If you believe I am wrong, tell me, with evidence to prove your position. I welcome the corrections. I may not respond, but I do promise to read and examine your arguments.

This has been an honest attempt to be an objective review of the objective and some subjective evidence. The exercise was not begun with the notion that it would absolutely, unequivocally prove or disprove that the United States was or was not founded as a Christian nation. It was to, as we are reminded on every episode of the CSI series, to find the objective evidence and evaluate that evidence to the best of my ability without preconceived prejudices. 130 people provided me with what they considered objective evidence. That evidence was followed and was objectively evaluated and that evidence is clear. There appears to be a lack of critical thinking and listening, not just within the Christian conservative, fundamental or evangelical movements, but within the American political and social systems.

This is not a matter of religion, but a signal, at least to me, of a great problem of not emphasizing education and, more specifically, the art of critical thinking in our K-12 education system.

It is saying that when an adult playing any one of the children's games of baseball, football, basketball, et cetera, as a rookie is worth starting salaries ten-times higher than tenured teachers is ludicrous. It is saying when a college president makes half as much as the college's football coach, something is amiss. It is saying when science is placed secondary to myth, when religion is of more importance than government and the free will of the people being governed, when we can no longer question the words of our collective ministers, we have lost the American perspective of truth and justice. And all of these failures can be, at least in part, to the lack of teaching critical thinking and listening to our five-years olds.

It is my conclusion that none of the 130 proponents of the various Christian nation theories were not lying They were not purposely misleading, and were not creating or perpetuating propaganda. They were, for the most part, taking the word of others as truth, without verification and without research of leaders and trusted contemporaries. But this is not limited to the Christian faiths; we all doing the same thing, from atheists to Orthodox Zeusists.

We are told something by a trusted authority or leader and assume that it must be true. We are using our heads, but the mind can justify anything given time. We have lost the art of listening to our gut and our wanting to ask "Why?"

Chapter 13

Post Script

ఆఈఈఆ

The question of religion of presidential candidates persists today and with the continued discomfort displayed toward religions outside of the mainstream Christian beliefs, atheism is seen through the cruelest lens of all. The common "belief" is that atheists, Muslims and other non-Christian faiths are somehow aligned with the Devil. You should rest assured and take comfort to know that if an atheist were elected to the highest office of the land, human sacrifice would not be permitted regardless of belief. America has no need to worry about a sacrificial temple being constructed near Ground Zero.

With a small change in the history of discovery, America would be a different nation, if it existed at all. Imagine what life would be like in North America if the Chinese explorer Zheng He, who may have landed in the Pacific Northwest between 1421 and 1423, had settled and expanded eastwards as part of the Ming Dynasty. This discussion would be in Chinese and the primary religion of the New World could have been Islam, Zheng He's purported birth religion.[1] Our language would be Chinese.

Alternatively, if Leifur (Leif or "The Lucky") Eiríksson, founder of Iceland and son of Eirik the Red, had remained in North America in the year 1000 and expanded westward, we would be speaking in one of the Scandinavian languages and the Norse's gods would no longer be myths.[2, 3]

On the academic side, if you disagree with my assessments, interpretations, or conclusions, I welcome your well thought out and supported discussions. If you are angered because you disagree with my writing and cannot write a civil letter or email, please do not - your correspondence will be deleted or trashed. If you would like to continue this conversation, please tell me. If you liked or agreed with something I said, I look forward to your note - my ego, like yours, needs occasional stroking.

I hope this finds you well and in great spirits. Shalom, Salam, Peace.

Please send your comments or questions to:

ACN@InkandVoice.com

Referenced Documents

Here are five documents mentioned that few have read in their entirety. Each comes from multiple sources including the Library of Congress, the State of Massachusetts, the Smithsonian Institute, and the Pilgrim Hall Museum, among others.

The reason these are included is not to extend the book, but because these are documents that are rarely read by the general public. This, by the way, includes the Constitution of the United States and the Declaration of Independence, though not included here.

The Mayflower Compact is a bit short, but reading it in its entity gives a better grasp of the thoughts of William Bradford and his merry followers.

A copy of the "A Modell of Christian Charity" is also included. It is also quite long, so please remember that this was a sermon, not a document.

Also included the portion we have come to know as "The City upon the Hill" in its original old English. You will note the problems with translating English into English.

I find that people are amazed when reading Patrick Henry's "Give me liberty." To understand the sediment best, Henry started slowly and quietly and ended with a great crescendo.

As with other documents, speeches and letters, few have read the five stanzas of the "Defence of Fort McHenry." Reading the entire poem gives a better sense as to why the first stanza became the National Anthem.

Finally, you will find the Treaty of Tripoli. Again, this is a much quoted but rare read document. It is also the only document that is specific in its statement as to the American government as noted by the founders, for many in the Senate at the time were of the original 200-plus we now call collectively "The Founders of the United States."

The Mayflower Compact of 1620

IN THE NAME OF GOD, AMEN. We, whose names are underwritten, the Loyal Subjects of our dread Sovereign Lord King *James*, by the Grace of God, of *Great Britain, France,* and *Ireland,* King, *Defender of the Faith,* &c. Having undertaken for the Glory of God, and Advancement of the Christian Faith, and the Honour of our King and Country, a Voyage to plant the first Colony in the northern Parts of *Virginia*; Do by these Presents, solemnly and mutually, in the Presence of God and one another, covenant and combine ourselves together into a civil Body Politick, for our better Ordering and Preservation, and Furtherance of the Ends aforesaid: And by Virtue hereof do enact, constitute, and frame, such just and equal Laws, Ordinances, Acts, Constitutions, and Officers, from time to time, as shall be thought most meet and convenient for the general Good of the Colony; unto which we promise all due Submission and Obedience.

IN WITNESS whereof we have hereunto subscribed our names at *Cape-Cod* the eleventh of November, in the Reign of our Sovereign Lord King *James*, of *England, France,* and *Ireland,* the eighteenth, and of *Scotland* the fifty-fourth, *Anno Domini*; 1620.

Signers:

John Carver	Edward Tilley	Degory Priest
William Bradford	John Tilley	Thomas Williams
Edward Winslow	Francis Cooke	Gilbert Winslow
William Brewster	Thomas Rogers	Edmund Margesson
Isaac Allerton	Thomas Tinker	Peter Brown
Myles Standish	John Rigsdale	Richard Britteridge
John Alden	Edward Fuller	George Soule
Samuel Fuller	John Turner	Richard Clarke
Christopher Martin	Francis Eaton	Richard Gardinar
William Mullins	James Chilton	John Allerton
William White	John Crackstone	Thomas English
Richard Warren	John Billington	Edward Doty
John Howland	Moses Fletcher	Edward Leister

Stephen Hopkins   John Goodman

A Modell of a Christian Charity

GOD ALMIGHTY in His most holy and wise providence, hath so disposed of the condition of mankind, as in all times some must be rich, some poor, some high and eminent in power and dignity; others mean and in submission.

The Reason hereof:

1st Reason. First to hold conformity with the rest of His world, being delighted to show forth the glory of his wisdom in the variety and difference of the creatures, and the glory of His power in ordering all these differences for the preservation and good of the whole, and the glory of His greatness, that as it is the glory of princes to have many officers, so this great king will have many stewards, counting himself more honored in dispensing his gifts to man by man, than if he did it by his own immediate hands.

2nd Reason. Secondly, that He might have the more occasion to manifest the work of his Spirit: first upon the wicked in moderating and restraining them, so that the rich and mighty should not eat up the poor, nor the poor and despised rise up against and shake off their yoke. Secondly, in the regenerate, in exercising His graces in them, as in the great ones, their love, mercy, gentleness, temperance etc., and in the poor and inferior sort, their faith, patience, obedience etc.

3rd Reason. Thirdly, that every man might have need of others, and from hence they might be all knit more nearly together in the bonds of brotherly affection. From hence it appears plainly that no man is made more honorable than another or more wealthy etc., out of any particular and singular respect to himself, but for the glory of his Creator and the common good of the creature, man. Therefore God still reserves the property of these gifts to Himself as Ezek. 16:17, He there calls wealth, His gold and His silver, and Prov. 3:9, He claims their service as His due, "Honor the Lord with thy riches," etc. --- All men being thus (by divine providence) ranked into two sorts, rich and poor; under the first are comprehended all such as are able to live comfortably by their own means duly improved; and all others are poor according to the former distribution.

There are two rules whereby we are to walk one towards another: Justice and Mercy. These are always distinguished in their act and in their object, yet may they both concur in the same subject in each respect; as sometimes there may be an occasion of showing mercy to a rich man in some sudden danger or distress, and also doing of mere justice to a poor man in regard of some particular contract, etc.

There is likewise a double Law by which we are regulated in our conversation towards another. In both the former respects, the Law of Nature and the Law of Grace (that is, the moral law or the law of the gospel) to omit the rule of justice as not properly belonging to this purpose otherwise than it may fall into consideration in some particular cases. By the first of these laws, man as he was enabled so withal is commanded to love his neighbor as himself. Upon this ground stands all the precepts of the moral law, which concerns our dealings with men. To apply this to the works of mercy, this law requires two things. First, that every man afford his help to another in every want or distress.

Secondly, that he perform this out of the same affection which makes him careful of his own goods, according to the words of our Savior (from Matthew 7:12), whatsoever ye would that men should do to you. This was practiced by Abraham and Lot in entertaining the angels and the old man of Gibea. The law of Grace or of the Gospel hath some difference from the former *(the law of nature),* as in these respects: First, the law of nature was given to man in the estate of innocence. This of the Gospel in the estate of regeneracy. Secondly, the former propounds one man to another, as the same flesh and image of God. This as a brother in Christ also, and in the communion of the same

Spirit, and so teacheth to put a difference between Christians and others. Do good to all, especially to the household of faith. Upon this ground the Israelites were to put a difference between the brethren of such as were strangers, though not of the Canaanites.

Thirdly, the Law of Nature would give no rules for dealing with enemies, for all are to be considered as friends in the state of innocence, but the Gospel commands love to an enemy. Proof: If thine enemy hunger, feed him; "Love your enemies... Do good to them that hate you" (Matt. 5:44).

This law of the Gospel propounds likewise a difference of seasons and occasions. There is a time when a Christian must sell all and give to the poor, as they did in the Apostles' times. There is a time also when Christians (though they give not all yet) must give beyond their ability, as they of Macedonia (2 Cor. 8). Likewise, community of perils calls for extraordinary liberality, and so doth community in some special service for the church.

Lastly, when there is no other means whereby our Christian brother may be relieved in his distress, we must help him beyond our ability rather than tempt God in putting him upon help by miraculous or extraordinary means. This duty of mercy is exercised in the kinds: giving, lending and forgiving *(of a debt)*.

Question: What rule shall a man observe in giving in respect of the measure?

Answer: If the time and occasion be ordinary he is to give out of his abundance. Let him lay aside as God hath blessed him. If the time and occasion be extraordinary, he must be ruled by them; taking this withal, that then a man cannot likely do too much, especially if he may leave himself and his family under probable means of comfortable subsistence.

Objection: A man must lay up for posterity, the fathers lay up for posterity and children, and he is worse than an infidel that provideth not for his own.

Answer: For the first, it is plain that it being spoken by way of comparison, it must be meant of the ordinary and usual course of fathers, and cannot extend to times and occasions extraordinary. For the other place the Apostle speaks against such as walked inordinately, and it is without question, that he is worse than an infidel who through his own sloth and voluptuousness shall neglect to provide for his family.

Objection: "The wise man's eyes are in his head," saith Solomon, "and foreseeth the plague;" therefore he must forecast and lay up against evil times when he or his may stand in need of all he can gather.

Answer: This very Argument Solomon useth to persuade to liberality (Eccle. 11), "Cast thy bread upon the waters...for thou knowest not what evil may come upon the land." Luke 16:9, "Make you friends of the riches of iniquity..." You will ask how this shall be? Very well. For first he that gives to the poor, lends to the Lord and He will repay him even in this life an hundredfold to him or his. The righteous is ever merciful and lendeth, and his seed enjoyeth the blessing; and besides we know what advantage it will be to us in the day of account when many such witnesses shall stand forth for us to witness the improvement of our talent. And I would know of those who plead so much for laying up for time to come, whether they hold that to be Gospel Matthew 6:19, "Lay not up for yourselves treasures upon earth," etc. If they acknowledge it, what extent will they allow it? If only to those primitive times, let them consider the reason whereupon our Savior grounds it. The first is that they are subject to the moth, the rust, the thief. Secondly, they will steal away the heart: "where the treasure is there will your heart be also."

The reasons are of like force at all times. Therefore the exhortation must be general and perpetual, with always in respect of the love and affection to riches and in regard of the things themselves when any special service for the church or particular distress of our brother do call for the use of them; otherwise it is not only lawful but necessary to lay up as Joseph did to have ready upon such occasions, as the Lord (whose stewards we are of them) shall call for them from us. Christ gives us an instance of the first, when he sent his disciples for the donkey, and bids them answer the owner thus, "the Lord hath need of him." So when the Tabernacle was to be built, He sends to His people to call for their silver and gold, etc., and yields no other reason but that it was for His work. When Elisha comes to the widow of Sareptah and finds her preparing to make ready her pittance for herself and family, he bids her first provide for him, he challenges first God's part which she must first give before she must serve her own family. All these teach us that the Lord looks that when He is pleased to call for His right in any thing we have, our own interest we have must stand aside till His turn be served. For the other, we need look no further then to that of 1 John 3:17, "He who hath this world's goods and seeth his brother to need and shuts up his compassion from him, how dwelleth the love of God in him?" Which comes punctually to this conclusion: If thy brother be in want and thou canst help him, thou needst not make doubt of what thou shouldst do; if thou lovest God thou must help him.

Question: What rule must we observe in lending?

Answer: Thou must observe whether thy brother hath present or probable or possible means of repaying thee, if there be none of those, thou must give him according to his necessity, rather then lend him as he requires *(requests)*. If he hath present means of repaying thee, thou art to look at him not as an act of mercy, but by way of commerce, wherein thou art to walk by the rule of justice; but if his means of repaying thee be only probable or possible, then he is an object of thy mercy, thou must lend him, though there be danger of losing it. (Deut. 15:7-8): "If any of thy brethren be poor ... thou shalt lend him sufficient." That men might not shift off this duty by the apparent hazard, He tells them that though the year of Jubilee were at hand (when he must remit it, if he were not able to repay it before), yet he must lend him, and that cheerfully. It may not grieve thee to give him, saith He. And because some might object, why so I should soon impoverish myself and my family, he adds, with all thy work, etc., for our Savior said (Matt. 5:42), "From him that would borrow of thee turn not away."

Question: What rule must we observe in forgiving *(a debt)*?

Answer: Whether thou didst lend by way of commerce or in mercy, if he hath nothing to pay thee, thou must forgive, (except in cause where thou hast a surety or a lawful pledge). Deut. 15:1-2 --- Every seventh year the creditor was to quit that which he lent to his brother if he were poor, as appears in verse 4. "Save when there shall be no poor with thee." In all these and like cases, Christ gives a general rule (Matt. 7:12), "Whatsoever ye would that men should do to you, do ye the same to them."

Question: What rule must we observe and walk by in cause of community of peril?

Answer: The same as before, but with more enlargement towards others and less respect towards ourselves and our own right. Hence it was that in the primitive Church they sold all, had all things in common, neither did any man say that which he possessed was his own. Likewise in their return out of the captivity, because the work was great for the restoring of the church and the danger of enemies was common to all, Nehemiah directs the Jews to liberality and readiness in remitting their debts to their brethren, and disposing liberally to such as wanted, and stand not upon their own dues which they might have demanded of them. Thus did some of our forefathers in times of persecution in England, and so did many of the faithful of other churches, whereof we keep an honorable remembrance of them; and it is to be observed that both in Scriptures and latter stories of the churches that such as have been most bountiful to the poor saints, especially in those extraordinary times and occasions, God hath left them highly commended to posterity, as Zaccheus, Cornelius, Dorcas, Bishop Hooper, the Cutler of Brussels and divers others. Observe again that the Scripture gives no caution to restrain any from being over liberal this way; but all men to the liberal and cheerful practice hereof by the sweeter promises; as to instance one for many (Isaiah 58:6-9) "Is not this the fast I have chosen to loose the bonds of wickedness, to take off the heavy burdens, to let the oppressed go free and to break every yoke ... to deal thy bread to the hungry and to bring the poor that wander into thy house, when thou seest the naked to cover them ... and then shall thy light brake forth as the morning and thy health shall grow speedily, thy righteousness shall go before God, and the glory of the Lord shalt embrace thee; then thou shall call and the Lord shall answer thee," etc. And from Ch. 2:10 *(??)* "If thou pour out thy soul to the hungry, then shall thy light spring out in darkness, and the Lord shall guide thee continually, and satisfy thy soul in draught, and make fat thy bones, thou shalt be like a watered garden, and they shalt be of thee that shall build the old waste places," etc. On the contrary most heavy curses are laid upon such as are straightened towards the Lord and his people (Judg. 5:23), "Curse ye Meroshe ... because they came not to help the Lord." He who shutteth his ears from hearing the cry of the poor, he shall cry and shall not be heard." (Matt. 25) "Go ye cursed into everlasting fire," etc. "I was hungry and ye fed me not." (2 Cor. 9:6) "He that soweth sparingly shall reap sparingly."

Having already set forth the practice of mercy according to the rule of God's law, it will be useful to lay open the grounds of it also, being the other part of the Commandment and that is the affection from which this exercise of mercy must arise, the Apostle tells us that this love is the fulfilling of the law, not that it is enough to love our brother and so no further; but in regard of the excellency of his parts giving any motion to the other as the soul to the body and the power it hath to set all the faculties at work in the outward exercise of this duty; as when we bid one make the clock strike, he doth not lay hand on the hammer, which is the immediate instrument of the sound, but sets on work the first mover or main wheel; knowing that will certainly produce the sound which he intends. So the way to draw men to the works of mercy, is not by force of Argument from the goodness or necessity of the work; for though this cause may enforce, a rational mind to some present act of mercy, as is frequent in experience, yet it cannot work such a habit in a soul, as shall make it prompt upon all occasions to produce the same effect, but by framing these affections of love in the heart which will as naturally bring forth the other, as any cause doth produce the effect.

The definition which the Scripture gives us of love is this: Love is the bond of perfection. First it is a bond or ligament. Secondly, it makes the work perfect. There is no body but consists of parts and that which knits these parts together, gives the body its perfection, because it makes each part so contiguous to others as thereby they do mutually participate with each other, both in strength and infirmity, in pleasure and pain. To instance in the most perfect of all bodies: Christ and his Church make one body. The several parts of this body considered a part before they were united, were as disproportionate and as much disordering as so many contrary qualities or elements, but when Christ comes, and by his spirit and love knits all these parts to himself and each to other, it is become the most perfect and best proportioned body in the world (Eph. 4:15-16). Christ, by whom all the body being knit together by every joint for the furniture thereof, according to the effectual power which is in the measure of every perfection of parts, a glorious body without spot or wrinkle; the ligaments hereof being Christ, or his love, for Christ is love (1 John 4:8). So this definition is right. Love is the bond of perfection.

From hence we may frame these conclusions:

First of all, true Christians are of one body in Christ (1 Cor. 12). Ye are the body of Christ and members of their part. All the parts of this body being thus united are made so contiguous in a special relation as they must needs partake of each other's strength and infirmity; joy and sorrow, weal and woe. If one member suffers, all suffer with it, if one be in honor, all rejoice with it.

Secondly, the ligaments of this body which knit together are love.

Thirdly, no body can be perfect which wants its proper ligament.

Fourthly, All the parts of this body being thus united are made so contiguous in a special relation as they must needs partake of each other's strength and infirmity, joy and sorrow, weal and woe. (1 Cor. 12:26) If one member suffers, all suffer with it; if one be in honor, all rejoice with it.

Fifthly, this sensitivity and sympathy of each other's conditions will necessarily infuse into each part a native desire and endeavor, to strengthen, defend, preserve and comfort the other. To insist a little on this conclusion being the product of all the former, the truth hereof will appear both by precept and pattern. 1 John 3:16, "We ought to lay down our lives for the brethren." Gal. 6:2, "Bear ye one another's burden's and so fulfill the law of Christ."

For patterns we have that first of our Savior who, out of his good will in obedience to his father, becoming a part of this body and being knit with it in the bond of love, found such a native sensitivity of our infirmities and sorrows as he willingly yielded himself to death to ease the infirmities of the rest of his body, and so healed their sorrows. From the like sympathy of parts did the Apostles and many thousands of the Saints lay down their lives for Christ. Again the like we may see in the members of this body among themselves. Rom. 9 --- Paul could have been contented to have been separated from Christ, that the Jews might not be cut off from the body. It is very observable what he professeth of his affectionate partaking with every member; "Who is weak (saith he) and I am not weak? Who is offended and I burn not?" And again (2 Cor. 7:13), "Therefore we are comforted because ye were comforted." Of Epaphroditus he speaketh (Phil. 2:25-30) that he regarded not his own life to do him service. So Phoebe and others are called the servants of the church. Now it is apparent that they served not for wages, or by constraint, but out of love. The like we shall find in the histories of the church, in all ages; the sweet sympathy of affections which was in the members of this body one towards another; their cheerfulness in serving and suffering together; how liberal they were without repining, harborers without grudging, and helpful without reproaching; and all from hence, because they had fervent love amongst them; which only makes the practice of mercy constant and easy.

The next consideration is how this love comes to be wrought. Adam in his first estate was a perfect model of mankind in all their generations, and in him this love was perfected in regard of the habit. But Adam, himself rent from his Creator, rent all his posterity also one from another; whence it comes that every man is born with this principle in him to love and seek himself only, and thus a man continueth till Christ comes and takes possession of the soul and infuseth another principle, love to God and our brother, and this latter having continual supply from Christ, as the head and root by which he is united, gets predominant in the soul, so by little and little expels the former. 1 John 4:7 --- Love cometh of God and every one that loveth is born of God, so that this love is the fruit of the new birth, and none can have it but the new creature. Now when this quality is thus formed in the souls of men, it works like the Spirit upon the dry bones. Ezek. 37:7 --- "Bone came to bone." It gathers together the scattered bones, or perfect old man Adam, and knits them into one body again in Christ, whereby a man is become again a living soul.

The third consideration is concerning the exercise of this love, which is twofold, inward or outward. The outward hath been handled in the former preface of this discourse. From unfolding the other we must take in our way that maxim of philosophy, "simile simili gaudet," or like will to like; for as of things which are turned with disaffection to each other, the ground of it is from a dissimilitude or arising from the contrary or different nature of the things themselves; for the ground of love is an apprehension of some resemblance in the things loved to that which affects it. This is the cause why the Lord loves the creature, so far as it hath any of his Image in it; He loves his elect because they are like Himself, He beholds them in His beloved son.

So a mother loves her child, because she thoroughly conceives a resemblance of herself in it. Thus it is between the members of Christ; each discerns, by the work of the Spirit, his own Image and resemblance in another, and therefore cannot but love him as he loves himself. Now when the soul, which is of a sociable nature, finds anything like to itself, it is like Adam when Eve was brought to him. She must be one with himself. This is flesh of my flesh (saith he) and bone of my bone. So the soul conceives a great delight in it; therefore she desires nearness and familiarity with it. She hath a great propensity to do it good and receives such content in it, as fearing the miscarriage of her beloved, she bestows it in the inmost closet of her heart. She will not endure that it shall want any good which she can give it. If by occasion she be withdrawn from the company of it, she is still looking towards the place where she left her beloved. If she heard it groan, she is with it presently. If she find it sad and disconsolate, she sighs and moans with it. She hath no such joy as to see her beloved merry and thriving. If she see it wronged, she cannot hear it without passion. She sets no bounds to her affections, nor hath any thought of reward. She finds recompense enough in the exercise of her love towards it.

We may see this acted to life in Jonathan and David. Jonathan a valiant man endued with the spirit of love, so soon as he discovered the same spirit in David had presently his heart knit to him by this ligament of love; so that it is said he loved him as his own soul, he takes so great pleasure in him, that he strips himself to adorn his beloved. His father's kingdom was not so precious to him as his beloved David, David shall have it with all his heart. Himself desires no more but that he may be near to him to rejoice in his good. He chooseth to converse with him in the wilderness even to the hazard of his own life, rather than with the great Courtiers in his father's Palace. When he sees danger towards him, he spares neither rare pains nor peril to direct it. When injury was offered his beloved David, he would not bear it, though from his own father. And when they must part for a season only, they thought their hearts would have broke for sorrow, had not their affections found vent by abundance of tears. Other instances might be brought to show the nature of this affection; as of Ruth and Naomi, and many others; but this truth is cleared enough. If any shall object that it is not possible that love shall be bred or upheld without hope of requital, it is granted; but that is not our cause; for this love is always under reward. It never gives, but it always receives with advantage:

First in regard that among the members of the same body, love and affection are reciprocal in a most equal and sweet kind of commerce.

Secondly, in regard of the pleasure and content that the exercise of love carries with it, as we may see in the natural body. The mouth is at all the pains to receive and mince the food which serves for the nourishment of all the other parts of the body; yet it hath no cause to complain; for first the other parts send back, by several passages, a due proportion of the same nourishment, in a better form for the strengthening and comforting the mouth. Secondly, the labor of the mouth is accompanied with such pleasure and content as far exceeds the pains it takes. So is it in all the labor of love among Christians. The party loving, reaps love again, as was showed before, which the soul covets more then all the wealth in the world.

Thirdly, nothing yields more pleasure and content to the soul then when it finds that which it may love fervently; for to love and live beloved is the soul's paradise both here and in heaven. In the State of wedlock there be many comforts to learn out of the troubles of that condition; but let such as have tried the most, say if there be any sweetness in that condition comparable to the exercise of mutual love.

From the former considerations arise these conclusions:

First, this love among Christians is a real thing, not imaginary.

Secondly, this love is as absolutely necessary to the being of the body of Christ, as the sinews and other ligaments of a natural body are to the being of that body.

Thirdly, this love is a divine, spiritual, nature; free, active, strong, courageous, permanent; undervaluing all things beneath its proper object and of all the graces, this makes us nearer to resemble the virtues of our heavenly father.

Fourthly, it rests in the love and welfare of its beloved. For the full certain knowledge of those truths concerning the nature, use, and excellency of this grace, that which the holy ghost hath left recorded, 1 Cor. 13, may give full satisfaction, which is needful for every true member of this lovely body of the Lord Jesus, to work upon their hearts by prayer, meditation continual exercise at least of the special influence of this grace, till Christ be formed in them and they in him, all in each other, knit together by this bond of love.

It rests now to make some application of this discourse, by the present design, which gave the occasion of writing of it. Herein are four things to be propounded; first the persons, secondly, the work, thirdly the end, fourthly the means.

First, for the persons. We are a company professing ourselves fellow members of Christ, in which respect only, though we were absent from each other many miles, and had our employments as far distant, yet we ought to account ourselves knit together by this bond of love and live in the exercise of it, if we would have comfort of our being in Christ. This was notorious in the practice of the Christians in former times; as is testified of the Waldenses, from the mouth of one of the adversaries Aeneas Sylvius "mutuo ament pene antequam norunt" --- they use to love any of their own religion even before they were acquainted with them.

Secondly for the work we have in hand. It is by a mutual consent, through a special overvaluing providence and a more than an ordinary approbation of the churches of Christ, to seek out a place of cohabitation and consortship under a due form of government both civil and ecclesiastical. In such cases as this, the care of the public must oversway all private respects, by which, not only conscience, but mere civil policy, doth bind us. For it is a true rule that particular estates cannot subsist in the ruin of the public.

Thirdly, the end is to improve our lives to do more service to the Lord; the comfort and increase of the body of Christ, whereof we are members, that ourselves and posterity may be the better preserved from the common corruptions of this evil world, to serve the Lord and work out our salvation under the power and purity of his holy ordinances.

Fourthly, for the means whereby this must be effected. They are twofold, a conformity with the work and end we aim at. These we see are extraordinary, therefore we must not content ourselves with usual ordinary means. Whatsoever we did, or ought to have done, when we lived in England, the same must we do, and more also, where we go. That which the most in their churches maintain as truth in profession only, we must bring into familiar and constant practice; as in this duty of love, we must love brotherly without dissimulation, we must love one another with a pure heart fervently. We must bear one another's burdens. We must not look only on our own things, but also on the things of our brethren.

Neither must we think that the Lord will bear with such failings at our hands as he doth from those among whom we have lived; and that for these three reasons:

First, in regard of the more near bond of marriage between Him and us, wherein He hath taken us to be His, after a most strict and peculiar manner, which will make Him the more jealous of our love and obedience. So He tells the people of Israel, you only have I known of all the families of the earth, therefore will I punish you for your transgressions.

Secondly, because the Lord will be sanctified in them that come near Him. We know that there were many that corrupted the service of the Lord; some setting up altars before his own; others offering both strange fire and strange sacrifices also; yet there came no fire from heaven, or other sudden judgment upon them, as did upon Nadab and Abihu, whom yet we may think did not sin presumptuously.

Thirdly, when God gives a special commission He looks to have it strictly observed in every article; When He gave Saul a commission to destroy Amaleck, He indented with him upon certain articles, and because he failed in one of the least, and that upon a fair pretense, it lost him the kingdom, which should have been his reward, if he had observed his commission.

Thus stands the cause between God and us. We are entered into covenant with Him for this work. We have taken out a commission. The Lord hath given us leave to draw our own articles. We have professed to enterprise these and those accounts, upon these and those ends. We have hereupon besought Him of favor and blessing. Now if the Lord shall please to hear us, and bring us in peace to the place we desire, then hath He ratified this covenant and sealed our commission, and will expect a strict performance of the articles contained in it; but if we shall neglect the observation of these articles which are the ends we have propounded, and, dissembling with our God, shall fall to embrace this present world and prosecute our carnal intentions, seeking great things for ourselves and our posterity, the Lord will surely break out in wrath against us, and be revenged of such a people, and make us know the price of the breach of such a covenant.

Now the only way to avoid this shipwreck, and to provide for our posterity, is to follow the counsel of Micah, to do justly, to love mercy, to walk humbly with our God. For this end, we must be knit together, in this work, as one man. We must entertain each other in brotherly affection. We must be willing to abridge ourselves of our superfluities, for the supply of others' necessities. We must uphold a familiar commerce together in all meekness, gentleness, patience and liberality. We must delight in each other; make others' conditions our own; rejoice together, mourn together, labor and suffer together, always having before our eyes our commission and community in the work, as members of the same body. So shall we keep the unity of the spirit in the bond of peace. The Lord will be our God, and delight to dwell among us, as His own people, and will command a blessing upon us in all our ways, so that we shall see much more of His wisdom, power, goodness and truth, than formerly we have been acquainted with. We shall find that the God of Israel is among us, when ten of us shall be able to resist a thousand of our enemies; when He shall make us a praise and glory that men shall say of succeeding plantations, "may the Lord make it like that of New England." For we must consider that we shall be as a city upon a hill. The eyes of all people are upon us. So that if we shall deal falsely with our God in this work we have undertaken, and so cause Him to withdraw His present help from us, we shall be made a story and a by-word through the world. We shall open the mouths of enemies to speak evil of the ways of God, and all professors for God's sake. We shall shame the faces of many of God's worthy servants, and cause their prayers to be turned into curses upon us till we be consumed out of the good land whither we are going.

And to shut this discourse with that exhortation of Moses, that faithful servant of the Lord, in his last farewell to Israel, Deut. 30. "Beloved, there is now set before us life and death, good and evil," in that we are commanded this day to love the Lord our God, and to love one another, to walk in his ways and to keep his Commandments and his ordinance and his laws, and the articles of our Covenant with Him, that we may live and be multiplied, and that the Lord our God may bless us in the land whither we go to possess it. But if our hearts shall turn away, so that we will not obey, but shall be seduced, and worship other Gods, our pleasure and profits, and serve them; it is propounded unto us this day, we shall surely perish out of the good land whither we pass over this vast sea to possess it.

Therefore let us choose life,

that we and our seed may live,

by obeying His voice and cleaving to Him,

for He is our life and our prosperity.

City Upon a Hill (ORIGINAL LANGUAGE AND SPELLING)

Now the onely way to avoyde this shipwracke and to provide for our posterity is to followe the Counsell of Micah, to doe Justly, to love mercy, to walke humbly with our God, for this end, wee must be knitt together in this worke as one man, wee must entertaine each other in brotherly Affeccion, wee must be willing to abridge our selves of our superfluities, for the supply of others necessities, wee must uphold a familiar Commerce together in all meekenes, gentlenes, patience and liberallity, wee must delight in eache other, make others Condicions our owne rejoyce together, mourne together, labour, and suffer together, allwayes haveing before our eyes our Commission and Community in the worke, our Community as members of the same body, soe shall wee keepe the unitie of the spirit in the bond of peace, the Lord will be our God and delight to dwell among us, as his owne people and will commaund a blessing upon us in all our wayes, soe that wee shall see much more of his wisdome power goodnes and truthe then formerly wee have beene acquainted with, wee shall finde that the God of Israell is among us, when tenn of us shall be able to resist a thousand of our enemies, when hee shall make us a prayse and glory, that men shall say of succeeding plantacions: the lord make it like that of New England: for wee must Consider that wee shall be as a Citty upon a Hill, the eies of all people are uppon us; soe that if wee shall deale falsely with our god in this worke wee have undertaken and soe cause him to withdrawe his present help from us, wee shall be made a story and a byword through the world, wee shall open the mouthes of enemies to speake evill of the wayes of god and all professours for Gods sake; wee shall shame the faces of many of gods worthy servants, and cause theire prayers to be turned into Cursses upon us till wee be consumed out of the good land whether wee are going: And to shutt upp this discourse with that exhortacion of Moses that faithfull servant of the Lord in his last farewell to Israell Deut. 30. Beloved there is now sett before us life, and good, deathe and evill in that wee are Commaunded this day to love the Lord our God, and to love one another to walke in his wayes and to keepe his Commaundements and his Ordinance, and his lawes, and the Articles of our Covenant with him that wee may live and be multiplyed, and that the Lord our God may blesse us in the land whether wee goe to possesse it: But if our heartes shall turne away soe that wee will not obey, but shall be seduced and worshipp other Gods our pleasures, and proffitts, and serve them, it is propounded unto us this day, wee shall surely perish out of the good Land whether wee passe over this vast Sea to possesse it;

> Therefore lett us choose life,
>
> that wee, and our Seede,
>
> may live; by obeyeing his
>
> voyce, and cleaveing to him,
>
> for hee is our life, and
>
> our prosperity.

Patrick Henry's "Give me liberty or give me death"
St. John's Church, Richmond, Virginia   March 23, 1775. [214]

MR. PRESIDENT: No man thinks more highly than I do of the patriotism, as well as abilities, of the very worthy gentlemen who have just addressed the House. But different men often see the same subject in different lights; and, therefore, I hope it will not be thought disrespectful to those gentlemen if, entertaining as I do, opinions of a character very opposite to theirs, I shall speak forth my sentiments freely, and without reserve. This is no time for ceremony. The question before the House is one of awful moment to this country. For my own part, I consider it as nothing less than a question of freedom or slavery; and in proportion to the magnitude of the subject ought to be the freedom of the debate. It is only in this way that we can hope to arrive at truth, and fulfil the great responsibility which we hold to God and our country. Should I keep back my opinions at such a time, through fear of giving offence, I should consider myself as guilty of treason towards my country, and of an act of disloyalty toward the majesty of heaven, which I revere above all earthly kings.

Mr. President, it is natural to man to indulge in the illusions of hope. We are apt to shut our eyes against a painful truth, and listen to the song of that siren till she transforms us into beasts. Is this the part of wise men, engaged in a great and arduous struggle for liberty? Are we disposed to be of the number of those who, having eyes, see not, and, having ears, hear not, the things which so nearly concern their temporal salvation? For my part, whatever anguish of spirit it may cost, I am willing to know the whole truth; to know the worst, and to provide for it.

I have but one lamp by which my feet are guided; and that is the lamp of experience. I know of no way of judging of the future but by the past. And judging by the past, I wish to know what there has been in the conduct of the British ministry for the last ten years, to justify those hopes with which gentlemen have been pleased to solace themselves, and the House? Is it that insidious smile with which our petition has been lately received? Trust it not, sir; it will prove a snare to your feet. Suffer not yourselves to be betrayed with a kiss. Ask yourselves how this gracious reception of our petition comports with these war-like preparations which cover our waters and darken our land. Are fleets and armies necessary to a work of love and reconciliation? Have we shown ourselves so unwilling to be reconciled, that force must be called in to win back our love? Let us not deceive ourselves, sir. These are the implements of war and subjugation; the last arguments to which kings resort. I ask, gentlemen, sir, what means this martial array, if its purpose be not to force us to submission? Can gentlemen assign any other possible motive for it? Has Great Britain any enemy, in this quarter of the world, to call for all this accumulation of navies and armies? No, sir, she has none. They are meant for us; they can be meant for no other. They are sent over to bind and rivet upon us those chains which the British ministry have been so long forging. And what have we to oppose to them? Shall we try argument? Sir, we have been trying that for the last ten years. Have we anything new to offer upon the subject? Nothing. We have held the subject up in every light of which it is capable; but it has been all in vain. Shall we resort to entreaty and humble supplication? What terms shall we find which have not been already exhausted? Let us not, I beseech you, sir, deceive ourselves. Sir, we have done everything that could be done, to avert the storm which is now coming on. We have petitioned; we have remonstrated; we have supplicated; we have prostrated ourselves before the throne, and have implored its interposition to arrest the tyrannical hands of the ministry and Parliament. Our petitions have been slighted; our remonstrances have produced additional violence and insult; our supplications have been disregarded; and we have been spurned, with contempt, from the foot of the throne. In vain, after these things, may we indulge the fond hope of peace and reconciliation. There is no longer any room for hope. If we wish to be free, if we mean to preserve inviolate those inestimable privileges for which we have been so long contending—if we mean not basely to abandon the noble struggle in which we have been so long engaged, and which we have pledged ourselves never to abandon until the glorious object of our contest shall be obtained, we must fight! I repeat it, sir, we must fight! An appeal to arms and to the God of Hosts is all that is left us!

They tell us, sir, that we are weak; unable to cope with so formidable an adversary. But when shall we be stronger? Will it be the next week, or the next year? Will it be when we are totally disarmed, and when a British guard shall be stationed in every house? Shall we gather strength by irresolution and inaction? Shall we acquire the means of effectual resistance, by lying supinely on our backs, and hugging the delusive phantom of hope, until our enemies shall have bound us hand and foot? Sir, we are not weak if we make a proper use of those means which the God of nature hath placed in our power. Three millions of people, armed in the holy cause of liberty, and in such a country as that which we possess, are invincible by any force which our enemy can send against us. Besides, sir, we shall not fight our battles alone. There is a just God who presides over the destinies of nations; and who will raise up friends to fight our battles for us. The battle, sir, is not to the strong alone; it is to the vigilant, the active, the brave. Besides, sir, we have no election. If we were base enough to desire it, it is now too late to retire from the contest. There is no retreat but in submission and slavery! Our chains are forged! Their clanking may be heard on the plains of Boston! The war is inevitable—and let it come! I repeat it, sir, let it come.

It is in vain, sir, to extenuate the matter. Gentlemen may cry, Peace, Peace—but there is no peace. The war is actually begun! The next gale that sweeps from the north will bring to our ears the clash of resounding arms! Our brethren are already in the field! Why stand we here idle? What is it that gentlemen wish? What would they have? Is life so dear, or peace so sweet, as to be purchased at the price of chains and slavery? Forbid it, Almighty God! I know not what course others may take; but as for me, give me liberty or give me death!

The Defense of Fort McHenry, Francis Scott Key, 1814

Oh, say can you see by the dawn's early light
What so proudly we hailed at the twilight's last gleaming?
Whose broad stripes and bright stars thru the perilous fight,
O'er the ramparts we watched were so gallantly streaming?
And the rocket's red glare, the bombs bursting in air,
Gave proof through the night that our flag was still there.
Oh, say does that star-spangled banner yet wave
O'er the land of the free and the home of the brave?

On the shore, dimly seen through the mists of the deep,
Where the foe's haughty host in dread silence reposes,
What is that which the breeze, o'er the towering steep,
As it fitfully blows, half conceals, half discloses?
Now it catches the gleam of the morning's first beam,
In full glory reflected now shines in the stream:
'Tis the star-spangled banner! Oh long may it wave
O'er the land of the free and the home of the brave!

And where is that band who so vauntinglyswore
That the havoc of war and the battle's confusion,
A home and a country should leave us no more!
Their blood has washed out their foul footsteps' pollution.
No refuge could save the hireling and slave
From the terror of flight, or the gloom of the grave:
And the star-spangled banner in triumph doth wave
O'er the land of the free and the home of the brave!

Oh! thus be it ever, when freemen shall stand
Between their loved home and the war's desolation!
Blest with victory and peace, may the heav'n rescued land

Praise the Power that hath made and preserved us a nation.
Then conquer we must, when our cause it is just,
And this be our motto: "In God is our trust."
And the star-spangled banner in triumph shall wave
O'er the land of the free and the home of the brave!

Treaty of Peace and Friendship between the United States of America and the Bey and Subjects of Tripoli of Barbary.

ARTICLE 1. - There is a firm and perpetual Peace and friendship between the United States of America and the Bey and subjects of Tripoli of Barbary, made by the free consent of both parties, and guaranteed by the most potent Dey & regency of Algiers.

ARTICLE 2. - If any goods belonging to any nation with which either of the parties is at war shall be loaded on board of vessels belonging to the other party they shall pass free, and no attempt shall be made to take or detain them.

ARTICLE 3. - If any citizens, subjects or effects belonging to either party shall be found on board a prize vessel taken from an enemy by the other party, such citizens or subjects shall be set at liberty, and the effects restored to the owners.

ARTICLE 4. - Proper passports are to be given to all vessels of both parties, by which they are to be known. And, considering the distance between the two countries, eighteen months from the date of this treaty shall be allowed for procuring such passports. During this interval the other papers belonging to such vessels shall be sufficient for their protection.

ARTICLE 5 - A citizen or subject of either party having bought a prize vessel condemned by the other party or by any other nation, the certificate of condemnation and bill of sale shall be a sufficient passport for such vessel for one year; this being a reasonable time for her to procure a proper passport.

ARTICLE 6 - Vessels of either party putting into the ports of the other and having need of provissions or other supplies, they shall be furnished at the market price. And if any such vessel shall so put in from a disaster at sea and have occasion to repair, she shall be at liberty to land and reembark her cargo without paying any duties. But in no case shall she be compelled to land her cargo.

ARTICLE 7. - Should a vessel of either party be cast on the shore of the other, all proper assistance shall be given to her and her people; no pillage shall be allowed; the property shall remain at the disposition of the owners, and the crew protected and succoured till they can be sent to their country.

ARTICLE 8. - If a vessel of either party should be attacked by an enemy within gun-shot of the forts of the other she shall be defended as much as possible. If she be in port she shall not be seized or attacked when it is in the power of the other party to protect her. And when she proceeds to sea no enemy shall be allowed to pursue her from the same port within twenty four hours after her departure.

ARTICLE 9. - The commerce between the United States and Tripoli,- the protection to be given to merchants, masters of vessels and seamen,- the reciprocal right of establishing consuls in each country, and the privileges, immunities and jurisdictions to be enjoyed by such consuls, are declared to be on the same footing with those of the most favoured nations respectively.

ARTICLE 10. - The money and presents demanded by the Bey of Tripoli as a full and satisfactory consideration on his part and on the part of his subjects for this treaty of perpetual peace and friendship are acknowledged to have been recieved by him previous to his signing the same, according to a reciept which is hereto annexed, except such part as is promised on the part of the United States to be delivered and paid by them on the arrival of their Consul in Tripoly, of which part a note is likewise hereto annexed. And no presence of any periodical tribute or farther payment is ever to be made by either party.

ARTICLE 11. - As the government of the United States of America is not in any sense founded on the Christian Religion,-as it has in itself no character of enmity against the laws, religion or tranquility of Musselmen,-and as the said States never have entered into any war or act of hostility against any Mehomitan nation, it is declared by the parties that no pretext arising from religious opinions shall ever produce an interruption of the harmony existing between the two countries.

ARTICLE 12. - In case of any dispute arising from a notation of any of the articles of this treaty no appeal shall be made to arms, nor shall war be declared on any pretext whatever. But if the (consul residing at the place where the dispute shall happen shall not be able to settle the same, an amicable referrence shall be made to the mutual friend of the parties, the Dey of Algiers, the parties hereby engaging to abide by his decision. And he by virtue of his signature to this treaty engages for himself and successors to declare the justice of the case according to the true interpretation of the treaty, and to use all the means in his power to enforce the observance of the same.

Signed and sealed at Tripoli of Barbary the 3d day of Jumad in the year of the Higera 1211-corresponding with the 4th day of Novr 1796 by

> JUSSUF BASHAW MAHOMET Bey
> SOLIMAN Kaya
> MAMET Treasurer
> GALIL Genl of the Troops
> AMET Minister of Marine
> MAHOMET Coml of the city
> AMET Chamberlain
> MAMET Secretary
> ALLY-Chief of the Divan

Signed and sealed at Algiers the 4th day of Argib 1211-corresponding with the 3d day of January 1797 by

HASSAN BASHAW Dey
and by the Agent plenipotentiary of the United States of America
[Seal] Joel BARLOW

Praise be to God &c-

The present writing done by our hand and delivered to the American Captain OBrien makes known that he has delivered to us forty thousand Spanish dollars,-thirteen watches of gold, silver & pinsbach,- five rings, of which three of diamonds, one of saphire and one with a watch in it, One hundred & forty piques of cloth, and four caftans of brocade,-and these on account of the peace concluded with the Americans.

Given at Tripoli in Barbary the 20th day of Jumad 1211, corresponding with the 21st day of Novr 1796-

(Signed) JUSSUF BASHAW-Bey whom God Exalt

ೞೲೲೞ

The foregoing is a true copy of the reciept given by Jussuf Bashaw- Bey of Tripoli-

(Signed) HASSAN BASHAW-Dey of Algiers.The foregoing is a literal translation of the writing in Arabic on the opposite page. JOEL BARLOW

ೞೲೲೞ

On the arrival of a consul of the United States in Tripoli he is to deliver to Jussuf Bashaw Bey-

>twelve thousand Spanish dollars
>five hawsers-8 Inch
>three cables-10 Inch
>twenty five barrels tar
>twenty five dÂ° pitch
>ten dÂ° rosin
>five hundred pine boards
>five hundred oak dÂ°
>ten masts (without any measure mentioned, suppose for vessels from 2 to 300 ton)
>twelve yards
>fifty bolts canvas
>four anchors

And these when delivered are to be in full of all demands on his part or on that of his successors from the United States according as it is expressed in the tenth article of the following treaty. And no farther demand of tributes, presents or payments shall ever be made.

Translated from the Arabic on the opposite page, which is signed & sealed by Hassan Bashaw Dey of Algiers-the 4th day of Argib 1211-or the 3d day of Jane 1797-by-Joel BARLOW

ঙ৪০৪০৩

To all to whom these Presents shall come or be made known.

Whereas the Underwritten David Humphreys hath been duly appointed Commissioner Plenipotentiary by Letters Patent, under the Signature of the President and Seal of the United States of America, dated the 30th of March 1795, for negotiating and concluding a Treaty of Peace with the Most Illustrious the Bashaw, Lords and Governors of the City & Kingdom of Tripoli; whereas by a Writing under his Hand and Seal dated the 10th of February 1796, he did (in conformity to the authority committed to me therefor) constitute and appoint Joel Barlow and Joseph Donaldson Junior Agents jointly and separately in the business aforesaid; whereas the annexed Treaty of Peace and Friendship was agreed upon, signed and sealed at Tripoli of Barbary on the 4th Of November 1796, in virtue of the Powers aforesaid and guaranteed by the Most potent Dey and Regency of Algiers; and whereas the same was certified at Algiers on the 3d of January 1797, with the Signature and Seal of Hassan Bashaw Dey, and of Joel Barlow one of the Agents aforesaid, in the absence of the other.

Now Know ye, that I David Humphreys Commissioner Plenipotentiary aforesaid, do approve and conclude the said Treaty, and every article and clause therein contained, reserving the same nevertheless for the final Ratification of the President of the United States of America, by and with the advice and consent of the Senate of the said United States.

In testimony whereof I have signed the same with my Name and Seal, at the City of Lisbon this 10th of February 1797.

    [Seal] DAVID HUMPHREYS.

Court Cases Cited

- Board of Education of the Westside Community Schools v. Mergens (496 U.S. 226 (1990))
- Cochran v. Louisiana, 281 U.S. 370
- Everson v. Board of Education of Ewing Township (NJ), 330 U.S. 1(1947)
- Everson v. Board of Education, 330 U. S. 1
- Holy Trinity v. US (143 U.S. 457)
- Minersville School District v. Gobitis, 310 U.S. 586 , 60 S.Ct. 1010, 127 A.L.R. 1493
- Mueller v. Allen, 463 U.S. 388 (1983)
- Muneer Awad v. Paul Ziriax, et al.
- People v. Ruggles (1811) 8 Johns R. 290 NY
- Rosenberger v. Rector and Visitors of the University of Virginia (515 U.S. 819 (1995))
- Torcaso v. Watkins, 367 U.S. 488 (1961)
- United States v. Macintosh, 283 U.S. 605 (1931)

- United States v. Schwimmer, supra, 279 U. S. 649-650, 279 U. S. 653

- Vidal vs. Girard's Executors (1844) 43U.S.127 2HOW.127 11L.ED.205

- West Virginia State Board of Education v. Bernette, 319 U.S. 624 (1943), 319 U.S. 624

Notes

A Christian Nation?

[1] Dewart, Deborah. *Death of a Christian Nation*. Chattanooga TN : AMG Publishers, 2010. Print.

[2] Hawking, Stephan, and Leonard Mlodinow. *The Grand Design*. New York, NY: Bantam Publishers, 2010. 42 - 51. Print.

In the Beginning

[1] Ronald Reagan. "Address to the National Religious Broadcasters Convention." American Rhetoric. . http://www.americanrhetoric.com/speeches/ronaldreagannrbroadcasters.htm

[2] I tell my students if they do not know the answer, ask a five-year old. They only think with their guts and have never heard that something cannot be done. They always seem to find an answer – sometimes in some strange boxes of their imagination.

[3] Simanek, Donald . "Bishop Ussher dates the world: 4004BC." http://www.lhup.edu/~dsimanek/ussher.htm (accessed January 5, 2011).

[4] Sagan, Carl. *A Demon Haunted World: Science as a Candle in the Dark*. New York, NY: Random House/Ballintine, 1996. Print.

[5] Fuller, R. Buckminster. *Operating Manual For The Spaceship Earth*. Boston: Lars M, 2009. Print.

[6] Sun Tzu, and James Clavell. *The Art of War*. New York, NY: Dell Publishing, 1983.

[7] United States Census Bureau, "Table 75. Self-Described Religious Identification of Adult Population: 1990 to 2008." Last modified 2011. Accessed

April 17, 2011.
http://www.census.gov/compendia/statab/2011/tables/11s0075.pdf

[8] The Universal Life Church itself has no creed and does not ask what religious denomination to which you belong. The membership also included atheists, Jews, Muslims, Buddhists and other religious communities.

[9] Reeves, Thomas. "Fulton J. Sheen, Catholic Campion." *FultonSheen.com*. . http://www.fultonsheen.com/Archbishop_Fulton_Sheen_biography.cfm.

[10] ibid

[11] *Army-McCarthy Hearings. McCarthyism*. Edited by Various. Wikipedia, http://en.wikipedia.org/wiki/Army–McCarthy_hearings.

[12] Reagan, Ronald. *Evil Empire. American Rhetoric*. http://www.youtube.com/watch?v=FcSm-KAEFFA.

[13] Whitburn, Joel. Billboard Book of Top 40 Hits. New York: Billboard, 1996.

[14] *The Founders' Constitution* Volume 1, Chapter 14, Document 10 http://press-pubs.uchicago.edu/founders/documents/v1ch14s10.html The University of Chicago Press

[15] Jews would not be included but for a religious reason. Some fundamentalist and evangelical Christians believe that Israel must survive if the Second Coming is to happen. That, again, is the subject of another book.

[1] CBSNews/AP, "Fire at Tenn. Building site ruled arson(2010), http://www.cbsnews.com/stories/2010/08/28/national/main6814690.shtml

[2] Article VI, clause 3 of the Constitution, "...but no religious Test shall ever be required as a Qualification to any Office or public Trust under the United States."

[3] Kennedy, John F. 1960. http://www.youtube.com/watch?v=ZmQCwXM9X6o

[4] Kennedy, John F. *Speech to the Greater Houston Ministerial Association. Presidential Rhetoric*. http://www.presidentialrhetoric.com/historicspeeches/kennedy/houstonministerial.html.

[5] Huckabee, Micheal. *Amend the Constitution to God's Standards*. Edited by Olbermann, Keith. New York: http://www.youtube.com/watch?v=Do8Dq_iNMRk&feature=related.

[6] Muneer Awad v. Paul Ziriax, et al.

[7] I will not make the argument here on the legality or constitutionality of the two Missouri HJRs. If you wish more information, please visit the Columbia Missourian http://www.columbiamissourian.com/stories/2011/03/16/david-rosman-keep-religion-out-government/

8 Poe, Catherine. "Jesus and Governor Perry." *The Washington Times*, sec. News, June 19, 2011.
http://communities.washingtontimes.com/neighborhood/ad-lib/2011/jun/19/jesus-and-gov-perry-winning-combo/

9 Jones, lawrance. "Rick Perry Deals with Critics."*Christian Post*, June 11, 2011.
http://www.christianpost.com/news/rick-perry-deals-with-criticism-over-prayer-rally-51090/

10 Lynn, Barry. "I am not a cowboy." *Americans United for Separation of Church and State*, June 22, 2011.
http://www.au.org/media/videos/archives/2011/not-a-cowboy.html?utm_source=au%2Bhomepage&utm_medium=homepage%2Bbanner&utm_campaign=Featured%2Bon%20homepage

11 Politically Incorrect, July, 1999
http://www.funnyordie.com/videos/be2c60b26d/christine-o-donnell-pi-july-19th-1999

12 O'Donnell, Christine. 2010.
http://www.youtube.com/watch?v=tGGAgljengs&feature=related

13 To speak of the Jews as a race is incorrect. To be Jewish concerns a person's religious affiliation as well as that person's heritage and tradition. The religion is said to pass through the maternal arms of the family. My mother, maternal grandmother, and her mother were Jewish, so, by tradition, I am a Jew. Jews come from every sector of the planet, including China. It is thought that the first Jews entered China in the 7th Century CE and mixed marriages were not uncommon. By the beginning of the Second World War, some eastern European Jews immigrated to Shanghai, China knowing of the Jewish community already established there. Today, there are some 1,500 known Chinese native Jews still living in Shanghai and the Ohel Rachel Synagogue in downtown was rededicated in 2010 after being closed for over 60 years.

Let's start with that Columbus guy

1 This was done in an attempt to avoid a lawsuit based on religious discrimination. It did not work.

2 "Books Ngram Viewer." *Google Labs*.
http://ngrams.googlelabs.com/graph?content=Christian+nation&year_start=1500&year_end=2010&corpus=0&smoothing=10

3 Ibid
http://ngrams.googlelabs.com/graph?content=Christian+Nation&year_start=1500&year_end=2008&corpus=0&smoothing=10

4 Richey, Warren. "Supreme Court: 'hurtful speech' of Westboro Baptist Church is protected." *The Christian Science Monitor*, March 02, 2011.
http://www.csmonitor.com/USA/Justice/2011/0302/Supreme-Court-hurtful-speech-of-Westboro-Baptist-Church-is-protected.

[5] Mooney, Chris. "The Science of Why We Don't Believe Science." *MotherJones*, may/June 2011. http://motherjones.com/politics/2011/03/denial-science-chris-mooney.

[6] Stolber, Sheryl Gay. New York Times, "For Bachman, God and Justice Were Intertwined." Last modified Oct 13, 2011. Accessed October 14, 2011. http://nytimes.com/2011/10/14/us/politics.

[1] Fongemie, Pauly. "Christopher Columbus." http://www.catholictradition.org/Tradition/christopher-columbus.htm

[2] Muhammad, Amir. "Muslims in America - Early History." 2005. http://www.muslimsinamerica.org/index.php?option=com_content&task=view&id=14&Itemid=29

[3] Mroueh, Youssef. "Muslims in America before Columbus." http://www.cyberistan.org/islamic/mamerica.html

[4] Fell, Barry. *Saga America*. New York, NY: Crown Publishing, 1983.

[5] Fitzpatrick-Matthews, Keith. "Barry Fell - Linguist genius or diluted amateur?" Apr. 9, 2007. http://www.badarchaeology.net/forgotten/barry_fell.php

[6] "Columbus' Muslim Captains." 2011. http://www.musalmantimes.com/?page_id=504

DEFINING "CHRISTIAN" AND FOUNDING.

[7] Maxwell, Richard and Pauly Howland. "Pilgrim Society Note, Series Two, March 2003." 03/2003. http://www.pilgrimhall.org/psnotenewpilgrimpuritan.htm

[8] Bradford, William. *Mayflower Compact of 1620*. Kindle Books. New York, NY: Amazon.com

[9] Winthrop, John. "Model of a Christian Nation." 1730. http://religiousfreedom.lib.virginia.edu/sacred/charity.html

[10] "Matthew 22." 1984.http://niv.scripturetext.com/matthew/22.htm

[11] ibid

[12] "Charter of Rhode Island and Providence Plantation." July 8, 1663.http://www.lonang.com/exlibris/organic/1663-cri.htm

[13] "Touro Synagogue." http://www.tourosynagogue.org/

[14] Seixas, Moses. "To Bigotry No Sanction." Aug. 17, 1790."Touro Synagogue." http://www.tourosynagogue.org/

[15] Washington, George. "To the Hebrew Congregation in Newport Rhode Island." 1791. http://www.tourosynagogue.org/pdfs/WashingtonLetter.pdf

[16] Rasmussen, Steven. "The Pagan Pilgrim." Nov. 21, 2001. http://www.oldenwilde.org/srasmus/oldentext/merrymount.html

[17] ibid

[18] http://www.georgia.gov/00/article/0,2086,4802_15177279_15252413,00.html

[19] *Set Apart: Religious Communities in Pennsylvania. ExplorePAHistory.* Harrisberg, PA: Commonwealth of Pennsylvania, http://explorepahistory.com/story.php?storyId=1-9-5.

[20] "A Brief History of New Sweden in America." *The Swedish Colonial society*, . http://www.colonialswedes.org/history/history.html

[21] "Dutch Colonies." *United States National Parks Service.* . http://www.nps.gov/history/nr/travel/kingston/colonization.htm

[22] Balmer, Randall. quoting J. Franklin Jameson, ed., *Narratives of New Netherland, 1609-1664* (New York, 1909), 123-125. *Religious diversity in America.Divining America*. Washington, DC: National Center for the Humanities, http://www.nationalhumanitiescenter.org/tserve/twenty/tkeyinfo/reldiv.htm.

[23] Balmer, Randall. "Calling New Yorkers to our better selves." *Columbia Spectator*, Sept 19, 2010. http://www.columbiaspectator.com/2010/09/19/calling-new-yorkers-our-better-selves.

[24] Della Rovere, Francesco. *Pope Sixtus IV. New Advent*. Catholic Excyclopedia,http://www.newadvent.org/cathen/14032b.htm

1

Who were these guys in wigs?

[1] The idea that there is a shared culture between Judaism and Christianity is not agreed to by many Jews of the United States. To the Orthodox Jew, even the shared "Books" of the two religious holy texts is a form of discontent.

[2] "Religion of the Founding Fathers of America." Dec. 7, 2005. http://www.adherents.com/gov/Founding_Fathers_Religion.html

[3] The Faiths of Our Founders: What America's Founders Really Believed. Lanham, Ma.: Rowman & Littlefield Publishing, 2003.

[4] Edited by J.D. Bowers, Peter Hughes, Dan McKanan, Jim Nugent, and Kathleen Parker . Boston: Unitarian Universalist Association, http://www25.uua.org/uuhs/duub/articles/thomasjefferson.html

[5] Jefferson, Thomas. "The Virginia Act for Establishing Religious Freedom - Religion Freedom Page." 1786. http://religiousfreedom.lib.virginia.edu/sacred/vaact.html

[6] Church, Forrest. "The Role of Religion in America." June 1, 2010. http://www.uua.org/visitors/uuperspectives/55665.shtml

[7] Jefferson, Thomas. *The Life and Morals of Jesus of Nazareth Extracted Textually from the Gospels*. Boston: Beacon Press, 1989.

[8] Jefferson, Thomas, ed. Arlington, VA: Bill of Rights Institute. "Letters between Thomas Jefferson and the Danbury Baptists (1802)." http://www.billofrightsinstitute.org/page.aspx?pid=517

[9] "Jefferson's Wall of Separation." June 1, 2010. http://www.usconstitution.net/jeffwall.html

[10] Jefferson, Thomas. "Letter to the Danbury Baptist Association." Jan. 1, 1802. http://www.loc.gov/loc/lcib/9806/danpost.html

[11] ibid p.29

[12] Franklin, Benjamin. "Requests Prayer in the Constitutional Convention." June 28, 1787. http://www.constitution.org/primarysources/franklin.html

[13] Franklin, Benjamin." June 28, 1787.

[14] Kidd, Thomas. *God of Liberty: A Religious History of the American Revolution*. New York, NY: Perseus Books, 2010. 116. Print.

[15] Harris, Samuel. "Letter to the President of the United States." http://unitedbaptists.org/UB%20letter%20to%20Washington.htm

[16] Washington, George. "Rediscovering George Washington - letter to the United Baptist Society of Virginia." May 10, 1789. http://www.pbs.org/georgewashington/collection/other_1789may10.html

[17] "George Washington and Religion." 1998. http://www.virginiaplaces.org/religion/religiongw.html

[18] Unger, H. (2010). *Lion of liberty: Patrick Henry and the Call to a New Nation*. Philadelphia: De Capo p19

[19] Ibid, p 21

[20] "The Religion of John Adams." Nov. 30, 2005. http://www.adherents.com/people/pa/John_Adams.html

[21] Mapp, Jr., Alf J. The Faiths of Our Fathers: What America's Founders Really Believed. Lantham, Ma.: Rowman & Littlefield, 2003. 41 - 53. Print.

[22] Ibid p.47

[23] Herron, Roy. God and Politics: How can a Christian be in Politics?. Carol Stream, IL: Tyndale House Publishers, 2005. vii. Print.

[24] Waldman, Steven. Founding Faith: How Our Founding Fathers Forged a Radical New Approach to Religious Liberty. New York, NY: Random House Trade Paperback, 2009. 228. Print.

[25] Adams, Letter to Jefferson, April 19,1817, quoted in Cappon, Adams-Jefferson Letters, 509.

[26] "The Religion of James Madison." Nov. 10, 2005.http://www.adherents.com/people/pm/James_Madison.html

[27] Mapp p. 48

[28] Mapp p. 49

[29] Mapp p. 49-50

[30] Congressional Record - House. Washington, DC: General Printing Office, 2001. Print. Comments made by Congressman Robert Wexler (D-Fla.)

[31] Mapp p. 51

[32] Madison, James. "Monopolies Perpetuities Corporations Ecclesiastical Endowments."

[33] Kreis, Steven. "Thomas Paine." Oct. 11, 2006.http://www.historyguide.org/intellect/paine.html

[34] Paine, Thomas. "Common Sense." http://www.ushistory.org/paine/commonsense/sense4.htm

[35] Paine, Thomas. "The Age of Reason." Jan. 27, 1794.http://libertyonline.hypermall.com/Paine/AOR-Frame.html

[36] ibid

[37] The Founders' Constitution. Volume 1, Chapter 2, Document 13. http://press-pubs.uchicago.edu/founders/documents/v1ch2s13.html

[38] Kramnick, Isaac, and R. Laurence Moore. The Godless Constitution: The Case Against Religious Correctness. New York, NY: W.W. Norton Publishing, 1997. 91. Print.

[39] Ressa, Keith T. "Christian Constitution." http://christianconstitutionalist.blogspot.com (This blog has been deleted in its entirety as of January 21, 2011)

[40] Phau, Donald. "HAMILTON'S FINAL YEARS: The Christian Constitutional Society." Jan. 1992.http://american_almanac.tripod.com/hamphau.htm

[41] Jay, William "The Life of John Jay" New York: J. & J. Harper, 183), Vol. II, p. 266, to Rev. Uzal Ogden, February 14, 1796

[42]
http://www.johnjayhomestead.org/images/The_Jays_and_Religion_for_website.pdf

What did they say?

[1] Stoll, Ira. Samuel Adams; A life. New York, NY: Free Press, a division of Simon & Schuster, 2008.

[2] Feinberg, Barbara S. the Articles of Confederation, the first constitution of the United States. Brookfield, Conn.: Millbrook Publishing, 2008.

[3] University of Virginia, "The Papers of George Washington." 2010.http://gwpapers.virginia.edu/

[4] Cited from Joseph Gales, Sr. compiler. The Debates and proceedings in the Congress of the United States; with an Appendix, Containing Important State Papers and Public Documents, and All the Laws of a Public Nature. (Annals of Congress.) 42 vols. Washington, D.C., 1834-1856, pp. 1:949-50.

[5] Propaganda in this case is an argument made primarily on emotion and extreme bias rather than facts in support or opposition to an organization, cause, doctrine or group.

[6] "Thanksgiving Proclamation." *Pilgrim Hall Museum.* 18 May 2005. Web. 24 Dec 2010. <http://www.pilgrimhall.org/GivingThanks3c.htm>.

[7] 36 USC Sec. 119

[8] *The History of Labor Day. United States department of Labor.* Washington, D.C.
http://www.dol.gov/opa/aboutdol/laborday.htm

[9] Carter, Jimmy. The American Presidency Project, "Jimmy Carter: Denver, Colorado Remarks at the Governor's Annual Prayer Breakfast Read more at the American Presidency Project: Jimmy Carter: Denver, Colorado Remarks at the Governor's Annual Prayer Breakfast. ." Accessed September 21, 2011. http://www.presidency.ucsb.edu/ws/index.php?pid=30748#ixzz1Yc9M3lHF.

The Founding Papers

[1] "Articles of Confederation." *U.S. Constitution Online.* USConstitution.net, Web. 25 Dec 2010. <http://www.usconstitution.net/articles.html>.

[2] Ibid Article II

[3] Washington Mss. (Papers of George Washington, Vol. 231); Library of Congress

[4] Library of Congress, "Religion and State Government." Jul. 23, 2010. http://www.loc.gov/exhibits/religion/rel05.html

[5] Madison, James. "Memorial and Remonstrance Against Religious Assessments." 1785.
http://religiousfreedom.lib.virginia.edu/sacred/madison_m&r_1785.html

[6] ibid, Paragraph 1

[7] ibid Paragraph 3

[8] Jefferson, Thomas. "The Virginia Act for Establishing Freedom of Religion." 1786.http://religiousfreedom.lib.virginia.edu/sacred/vaact.html

[9] Hamilton, Alexander, James Madison and John Jay. *The Federalist Papers.* Garry F. Wills. New York, NY: Bantam Books, 1982.
[10] Ibid p.50
[11] "The Polity of the Lacedaemonians."
http://ancienthistory.about.com/library/bl/bl_text_xenophon_lacedaemonians.htm.
[12] Wills p.77
[13] Ibid p.7
[14] Ibid p.314
[15] Ibid p.418
[16] http://www.fordham.edu/halsall/mod/Rousseau-soccon.html

[17] Locke, John. Two Treatises of Government. Student Edition ed. Raymond Geuss, Quentin Skinner. Cambridge, England: Cambridge University Press, 1988.

[18] Ibid p.216

[19] Ibid p. 267

[20] Grossman, Cathy Lynn . "No Proof Washington said "so help me God."." *USA Today*, Jan. 7, 2009

[21] U.S. Senate, Rules Committee, "Inauguration of the President: Facts and Firsts." http://inaugural.senate.gov/history/factsandfirsts/index.cfm

[22] U.S. Senate, Rules Committee, "Inauguration of President George Washington." http://inaugural.senate.gov/history/chronology/gwashington1789.cfm

[23] Taken from "Our Founding Fathers: Documents and Debates of religious Establishment" Council on Religious Freedom, Rockville MD, 1997

[24] Kennedy, Edward "Ted". "Faith, Truth and Tolerance in America." Oct. 3, 1983. http://americanrhetoric.com/speeches/tedkennedytruth&tolerance.htm

[25] Cornell University Law School, "First Amendment, Religion and Expression." http://www.law.cornell.edu/anncon/html/amdt1afrag1_user.html

[26] Rosman, David. "Atheists are a Protected Class. But a Religion?."*InkandVoice* (blog), Oct 16, 2011. http://inkandvoice.com/2011/10/atheists/ (accessed October 16, 2011).

[27] A member of the Church of the Flying Spaghetti Monster

[28] For more on current arguments concerning the exceptions to first Amendment freedoms of expression, see: Rosman, David. "How do we define journalist?."Columbia Missourian (2010). Web. 16 Dec 2010. <http://www.columbiamissourian.com/stories/2010/12/15/david-rosman-how-do-you-define-journalist-does-julian-assange-count/>.

God and the Constitution

[1] Brooks, Mel. "Moses - Ten Commandments." May, 2008. http://www.youtube.com/watch?v=4TAtRCJIqnk

[2] Lattin, Don. "Just which commandments are the 10 Commandments?" *San Francisco Chronicle*, August 26, 2003. http://articles.sfgate.com/2003-08-26/news/17503693_1_commandment-two-shalt-neighbor-s-wife

[3] King James Version

[4] King James Version (KJV)

[5] "The 613 Commandments." *Liberty Praise*. N.p., n.d. Web. 30 Dec 2010. <http://www.libertypraise.com/613laws/mandatory.pdf>.

[6] *Which Ten Commandments?. Positive Atheist*. Edited by Cliff Walker and Jyoti Shankar
http://www.positiveatheism.org/crt/whichcom.htm

[7] Dershowitz, Alan. *Rights From Wrongs: A Secular Theory of the Origins of Rights*. New York, NY: Basic Books, 2005.

[8] Having met and spoken with Dershowitz, I must disagree with that assessment.

[9] Wistrich, Robert S. *Who's who in Nazi German*. NY: Routledge Press, 1995.

[10] Jewish Virtual History, "Martin Niemoeller." 2010.
http://www.jewishvirtuallibrary.org/jsource/Holocaust/Niemoller_quote.html

[11] ibid.

[12] Lincoln, Abraham. *Gettysburg Address. American Rhetoric*. 1863.
http://www.americanrhetoric.com/speeches/gettysburgaddress.htm

[13] Kennedy, Edward. "Faith, Truth and Tolerance in America." Oct. 3, 1983.
http://www.americanrhetoric.com/speeches/tedkennedytruth&tolerance.htm

[14] As of this writing, new elections are slated for Turkey with Islamic partied vying for control of the parliament. Observers in Turkey have indicated to me through email that the possibility of Turkey becoming an Islamic nation is small, but the Islamic parties can become a driving factor in a correlation government and thus effecting the rule of law.

[15] Filer, Eddie. "Is the United States a Christian Nation?." *Naples Daily News* 03 Nov 2010: Web. 30 Dec 2010.
<http://www.naplesnews.com/blogs/social-critic/2010/nov/03/christian/>

In God We Trust

[1] The Smithsonian Institute, "Star-Spangled Banner and the War of 1812." Nov. 2004.
http://www.si.edu/encyclopedia_si/nmah/starflag.htm

[2] Library of Congress, "God Bless America." Jul 27, 2010.http://www.loc.gov/exhibits/treasures/trm019.html

[3] "E Pluribus Unum." Jul. 4, 2010.
http://www.greatseal.com/mottoes/unum.html

[4] Boy Scouts of America, "The Great Seal and National Mottos of the United States of America."
http://usscouts.org/flag/sealmotto.asp

[5] Freeman, Joanne . "Time Line of the Civil War."
http://memory.loc.gov/ammem/cwphtml/tl1861.html

[6] A search on Google labs' Ngram View using *"Christian Nation"* shows a substantial increased use between 1840s and 1890s. Decline of the term seems to continue, except during the period of World War II, Korea and Vietnam, until the 1980's, showing a substantial increase usage since.

[7] United States Treasury. "In God We Trust." http://www.ustreas.gov/education/fact-sheets/currency/in-god-we-trust.shtml

[8] ReligiousTolorance.org

[9] "Roosevelt Dropped "In God We Trust"." New York Times, Nov. 13, 1907

[10] ibid

[11] Nodia, Ghia. "Nationalism and Democracy." Democracy: A Reader. Ed. Richardo Blaug. New York: Columbia University Press, Print.

[12] *Longley, Robert, ed. About.com. "Brief History of the Pledge of Allegiance."* http://usgovinfo.about.com/cs/usconstitution/a/pledgehist.htm

[13] Lakoff, Shelley. "History of the Pledge of Allegiance." 2008. http://www.historyofthepledge.com

[14] Lakoff, Shelley

[15] Boren, Cindy. "NBC apologizes for cutting "Under God" in the Pledge." 06/19/2011.http://www.washingtonpost.com/blogs/early-lead/post/nbc-apologizes-for-cutting-under-god-from-pledge-of-allegiance-before-us-open/2011/06/19/AG8MgtbH_blog.html (accessed June 25, 2011).

[16] *The Battle of Gettysburg.* (2006, November 25). Retrieved from http://www.civilwarhome.com/gettysbu.htm

[17] LOC Exhibitions - Gettysburg Address. Retrieved from http://myloc.gov/Exhibitions/gettysburgaddress/Pages/default.aspx

[18] *Edward Everett's Gettysburg Address.* (1965, August 09). Retrieved from http://www.civilwarhome.com/everettgettysburg.htm

[19] LOC

[20] LOC

[21] Reckers, S. *Virtual Gettysburg -The Gettysburg Address.* Retrieved from http://www.virtualgettysburg.com/exhibit/lincoln/feature.html

[22] Smithsonian institute - The Gettysburg address. (2008, November 21). Retrieved from http://americanhistory.si.edu/documentsgallery/exhibitions/gettysburg_address_2.html

[23] Unruh, Bob. (2010). Now "under god" dropped from the Gettysburg Address. WorldNetDaily, Retrieved from http://www.wnd.com/?pageId=210701

[24] George, R. (2010, July). God and Gettysburg, Retrieved from http://www.firstthings.com/article/2010/07/god-and-gettysburg

[25] Debate or distraction: why some are fretting over the ACS Pocket Constitution. (2010, July 20). Retrieved from http://www.acslaw.org/acsblog/node/16548

[26] American Constitution Society. The declaration of independence, the Gettysburg address and the constitution of the United States of America.

Retrieved from
http://www.acslaw.org/files/ACS%20Pocket%20Constitution.pdf

[27] To read the ACS response to the George blog commentary, go to: http://www.acslaw.org/acsblog/node/16548. Ms. Caroline Fredrickson, Executive Director of ACS reputes the George and Unruh arguments that ACS manipulated the language of the Address as a plot.

Here come da Justices

[1] Marshall, John. "Marbury v. Madisonv.*Marbury v. Madison, 5 U.S. 1 Cranch 137 137 (1803)*". 5. (1803), 137-180, http://supreme.justia.com/us/5/137/case.html.

[2] "Church of the Holy Trinity v. United States, 143 U. S. 457 (1892)." Justia.com. U.S. Supreme court Center, Web. 24 Dec 2010. <http://supreme.justia.com/us/143/457/case.html>.

[3] "Title 8, Chapter 6, Subchapter 11." legal Information Institute. Cornell University School of Law, Web. 24 Dec 2010. <http://www.law.cornell.edu/uscode/8/usc_sec_08_00000137---b000-.html>

[4] This section was repealed June 27, 1952

[5] *Emerson v. Board of Education Ewing Township.* (n.d.). Retrieved from http://religiousfreedom.lib.virginia.edu/court/ever_v_boar.html

[6] People v. Ruggles 8 Johns. R. 290 N.Y. 1811. (2000).*The founder's constitution.* Retrieved December 24, 2010, from http://press-pubs.uchicago.edu/founders/documents/amendI_religions62.html

[7] The Supreme Court of New York State, 8 Johns R 291 NY

[8] United States. Vidal vs. Girard's Executors. Washington, DC: USSC, 1844. Print.

[9] Slavery in the North, "Racism in Pennsylvania." 2003.http://www.slavenorth.com/pennrace.htm

[10] Net Industries, "Vidal v. Girard's Executors." 2010.http://law.jrank.org/pages/11123/Vidal-v-Girard-s-Executors.html

[11] *Vidal, Francois Fenelon, John Girard, and others citizens and Subjects of the Monarchy of France, and Henry Stump, complainants and appellants, v. the Mayor, Aldermen and citizens of Philadelphia, the executors of Stephen Girard, and others, defendants* Jan. 1844. http://ftp.resource.org/courts.gov/c/US/43/43.US.127.html

[12] Ibid Law.jrank.org

[13] Sutherland, George. "U.S. v. Macintosh, 283 U.S. 605." may 25, 1931.http://caselaw.lp.findlaw.com/cgi-bin/getcase.pl?court=us&vol=283&invol=605

[14] University of Virginia, School of Law. "United States v. Macintosh." http://religiousfreedom.lib.virginia.edu/court/us_v_maci.html

[15] "Torcaso v. Watkins." *Justia.com*. N.p., n.d. Web. 25 Dec 2010. <http://supreme.justia.com/us/367/488/case.html>.

[16] Ibid

[17] State of North Carolina. *Constitution of the State of North Carolina.*, Web. 25 Dec 2010. <http://www.ncga.state.nc.us/Legislation/constitution/article6.html>.

[18] Neumeyer, George. "Obama's unholy war on Christianity, not Islam." American Spectator 08 Apr 2009: n. pag. Web. 25 Dec 2010. <http://spectator.org/archives/2009/04/08/obamas-unholy-war-against-chri>. This is an example of one of the more rabid columns found on the Internet.

[19] Limbaugh, David. Persecution: How Liberals are Waging War Against Christianity. New York, NY: Harper, 2004. Print.

[20] "Mueller v. Allen 463 US 388." Religious Freedom. University of Virginia. Web. 25 Dec 2010. <http://religiousfreedom.lib.virginia.edu/court/muel_v_alle.html>.

[21] "Cochran v. Louisiana 281 U.S. 370." Religious Freedom. University of Virginia. Web. 25 Dec 2010. <http://religiousfreedom.lib.virginia.edu/court/coch_v_loui.html>.

[22] *West Virginia State Board of Education v. Barnette, 319 U.S. 624 (1943) 319 U.S. 624.* West Law, 1943Washington, DC http://caselaw.lp.findlaw.com/scripts/getcase.pl?court=us&vol=319&invol=624

[23] Minersville School District v. Gobitis, 310 U.S. 586 (1940) 310 U.S. 586.WestLaw. *http://laws.findlaw.com/us/310/586.html*

[24] 319 U.S. 624, 627

[25] 310 U. S. 594, 595

[26] "Minersville School District v. Gobitis, 310 U.S. 586 (1940) 310 U.S. 586. WestLaw http://laws.findlaw.com/us/310/586.html

[27] Eisgruber, Christopher and Lawrence G. Sager. *Religious Freedom and the Constitution*. Cambridge, MA: Harvard University Press, 2007.

In the End

[1] Rosman, David. New York Journal of Books, "An Enlightened Philosophy: Can an Atheist Believe Anything?." Last modified April 16, 2011. Accessed April 17, 2011. http://www.nyjournalofbooks.com/review/enlightened-philosophy-can-atheist-believe-anything.

[2] "U.S. Religious Knowledge Survey." Pew Research Center . .
http://www.pewtrusts.org/news_room_detail.aspx?id=60976

[1] Hadingham, Evan. "Ancient Chinese Treasures." *NOVA Online / Sultan's Lost Treasures*. Web. 30 Dec 2010.
<http://www.pbs.org/wgbh/nova/sultan/explorers.html>.

[2] "Discovery of Greenland and America." Gateway to Iceland. Republic of Iceland, Web. 30 Dec 2010. <http://www.iceland.is/history-and-culture/History/Discovery-of-America/>.

[3] Many believe that Leif Eiriksson may have been a Christian. Christianity had already made headway in Viking society by the time of Eiriksson's birth, circa 970 C.E. However, the Nords gods were still prevalent during this time with one saga relating to Thor and Jesus in a battle for supremacy.

[214] Henry, Patrick. American Rhetoric, "Give me liberty or give me death."
http://www.americanrhetoric.com/speeches/patrickhenrygivemeliberty.html.

Made in the USA
Lexington, KY
26 January 2012